estherpress

Books for Courageous Women

ESTHER PRESS VISION

Publishing diverse voices that encourage and equip women to walk courageously in the light of God's truth for such a time as this.

BIBLICAL STATEMENT OF PURPOSE

"For if you keep silent at this time, relief and deliverance will rise for the Jews from another place, but you and your father's house will perish. And who knows whether you have not come to the kingdom for such a time as this?"

Esther 4:14 (ESV)

COME BACK TO GOD

AN INTERACTIVE BIBLE STUDY

Includes Six-Session Video Series

COME BACK TO GOD

Letting Go of What's Keeping You from Soul Revival

LISA WHITTLE

ep

estherpress

Books for Courageous Women
from David C Cook

COME BACK TO GOD
Published by Esther Press,
an imprint of David C Cook
4050 Lee Vance Drive
Colorado Springs, CO 80918 U.S.A.

Integrity Music Limited, a Division of David C Cook
Brighton, East Sussex BN1 2RE, England

ISBN 978-0-8307-8539-1
eISBN 978-0-8307-8540-7

The author is represented by Alive Literary Agency, www.aliveliterary.com.

The Team: Susan McPherson, Stephanie Bennett, Judy Gillispie, Renée Chavez,
James Hershberger, Susan Murdock, Angela Messinger
Cover Design: Emily Weigel

Printed in the United States of America
First Edition 2026

1 2 3 4 5 6 7 8 9 10

100625

To the church:
As flawed as we are, you gave me VBS, choir, Sunday school, potlucks, youth camp, and revival nights. I always came back to God because of my early years spent with you.
For this and many other reasons, I will always love you.

Contents

Session 4: More Than Popularity

Session 5: More Than Blessing

Session 6: Coming Back

Many Thanks ...

Thank you to Sarah Farish, someone who has once again made me consider the studier in this Bible study in a greater way. Your input on this project is invaluable.

Thank you to my awesome team at Esther Press—Susan, Stephanie, Luke, Judy, Renee, Spencer, and Isabelle (among others!). You are stellar and oh so genuinely likeable. Thank you.

To Lisa Jackson, Team LWM, and my fam team at home: Your support in the everyday is what helps me serve others. Thank you for your encouragement and belief, which strengthens my heart.

To Jesus ... only You and I know the times I've come back to You in my life. I'll never be able to offer enough thank-Yous for the open arms, every single time. I love You most, forever.

From the Heart of Lisa

Welcome and ... congratulations.

Welcome to this study, which I trust and pray will be fruitful for you.

Congratulations for saying yes—not to me or even to this study but to a pursuit of God. That's really what this study is.

I know it took courage to be here. It would be much easier to pretend your life is perfect and play church, as so many of us do year after year. But perfection is overrated, denial has never proven successful, and most of us are tired of never moving forward.

I'm excited for you because I know what God promises in His Word to people who seek Him with their whole heart. He says He will draw near. He says He will be found. He says that when we call out to Him, He will tell us things we do not yet know. All these things are pursuit worthy.

The insights, peace, and strength of the Lord in these difficult times are life and breath to our body and bones. I don't have to tell you that we need life breathed back into us.

So many of us are weary to the bone. We have learned how to develop better systems for getting rest, setting greater boundaries, learning new strategies to thrive. But our conversations with friends and loved ones remain the same. We cannot seem to get traction. We feel exhausted. We are not happy.

I am not promising you a magic pill in this study. I am extending to you some of my own personal process that has changed my life in the form of studying and teaching—things I believe will be important to you becoming revived in your own spirit.

Maybe you've always wanted to have a vibrant relationship with God, but you've never known how. Perhaps you've never even known how to articulate what you want out of life or, due to circumstances, what you want has gotten a bit fuzzier. Or perhaps you once had a close relationship with God, but other things have gotten in the way. He is beckoning you to come back.

In any case, I believe the Lord is going meet you in a powerful way in these pages.

I am praying for that and seeking Him with you.

I want God,

Lisa

Ways to Study *Come Back to God*

As followers of Christ, we all either have a desire for less of us and more of God or we *want* to have such a desire, and yet the difficulty we so often face is knowing how to get there. So I've broken down this Bible study for you into six parts of the process to spiritually coming alive.

Each of the six parts of the revival process is studied over the course of six sessions (or weeks), further broken down into five days. The first day involves watching the video and completing the accompanying outline (as a group), and the remaining days are completed on your own.

It Will Look Like This

Day 1 (group or on your own): *Video teaching with Lisa.* Start each session by watching the video and completing the outline. (Preferably together if you are group studying, but it can be done separately. See the Leader's Guide in the back for additional discussion/guidance in your group time.) There should be plenty for you to unpack from this lesson.

Day 2 (on your own): *What is my real issue?* Define the issue and gain more perspective and insight into what is happening in light of the gospel.

Day 3 (on your own): *What do I want?* Get more introspective/personal and think about the specific issue at hand (e.g., control, comfort, etc.) in the context of this question.

Day 4 (on your own): *What is in my way?* Identify the blockers—call out the idols.

Day 5 (on your own): *How can I have a soul revival?* Delve into the three key spiritual practices of remembrance, repentance, and repetition and put them into play for each issue at hand.

Try to complete the material for each day to keep up your momentum.

Come Back to God Can Be Studied Individually or as a Group

If you study *Come Back to God* as a group, your leader should guide the group. The Leader's Guide is in the back of the book for your convenience.

If you study *Come Back to God* individually, you will simply omit instructions to group leaders and engage with the entirety of material yourself. Consider sharing with your friends what you are learning!

Additional Tips for Personal Study

- On average, plan for each day's material to take thirty to forty-five minutes.
- Always start a new session by watching the video and using the outline for taking notes (with or without a group).
- The most effective flow is to follow the days in order.

Additional Tips for Leading Group Study

- Seek to keep every gathering at one to one and a half hours.
- Watch the video together, when at all possible. If not, have your group members watch on their own in advance and then pick up with discussion, per the Leader's Guide.

- Don't feel the burden of being each other's counselors. Offer counsel as the Lord leads, but encourage one another to seek professional help where needed.

More leader tips, as well as the full Leader's Guide, are in the back of this book.

Study Guide FAQs

How do we access the videos?

For your convenience, you can easily access the videos with your copy of the *Come Back to God* study guide. Check out the QR code (or link) on page 17 for streaming video access. Watch the corresponding video from your phone or computer to begin each session. If you're doing the study with a group, each participant will have access to all the video teachings with her study guide.

Do we need to buy the book *I Want God* to participate in the study?

No, the main book is optional. Although the study guide has been created to work independently, you're encouraged to also have a copy of my book *I Want God* because, together, they complete a fuller picture of how God can bring spiritual breakthrough in your life. Every session of the Bible study connects you to the coordinating chapter(s) of the book to help you get the most out of your study time.

What is the best way to memorize the recommended verses at the beginning of every session?

We highly suggest the Memory Verse Repetition Model for memorizing those verses.

1. Write down the verse on a note card or type it into your notes app.
2. Read the verse (including the reference) out loud five times.
3. Focus on one phrase of the verse and memorize it for two days, then the next phrase for two days, then the last phrase the last two days. Add on to the verse as you go along, saying the first phrase with the second phrase and so on.

Here are a few additional tips to increase the fun:

Create a hashtag for Instagram to easily share insights about the study with one another online. (Suggestions: #CBTGCharlotteSouth or a cute name that includes the name *Come Back to God* or the initials CBTG.) To find your hashtag group, hit the magnifying glass and type in the name, and it will come up!

Choose a "study sister" within the group to create one-on-one accountability. She can be your designated study partner—someone to check in with, practice the memory verses with, and share with about the things God is showing each of you.

Throw a dinner or party at the end of the study to celebrate your time together and what God has done among you and in you. Calendar it at the start, along with your other study dates, so you know when it is in advance, and plan for it. Make it special!

Session 1

REVIVAL

YOU ARE MY PLACE OF REFUGE. YOU ARE ALL I REALLY WANT IN LIFE.

Psalm 142:5b

Memorize this verse this week by our repetition model.

To follow along in the *I Want God* book, read chapters 1, 2, and 12.

DAY 1

Video and Outline

Stream the "Revival" (session 1) video (link on p. 17) and complete the session 1 outline below as you watch.

Group leaders: See the session 1 guide in the back (p. 189) for group discussion information.

- **Revivals are incredible ____________________.**
- **Revivals start inside the soul of someone who is coming to God for the first time or coming back to God with a __________ and ______________ heart.**
- **Revival isn't just about a corporate gathering. It's about what God does to bring you ______________.**
- **Desperation is often the exact ____________________ to be in to bring on needed revival.**
- **Cycle of longing:**

  1. **We have a ______________ for something.**
  2. **We ________ on the longing.**

3. We ______________ often temporary results that satisfy the longing.
4. We still long and either change our ______________ to something else ... or change our ______________ of getting the same longing in our ______________.

✦ Jesus Himself asked the very question "______________" in John 1—a question that went straight to longing.

✦ The word that is repeated three times in this passage (Matt. 22:37), *ALL*, tells us what kind of heart God wants. It's also the kind of life God wants from us and for us: ______________.

✦ If we don't want God the most, if He's not our primary longing, then today can start a new positioning: a heart that is ______________ and ______________ for revival.

✦ The benefit of knowing what you want: the complications of daily life decisions become ______________ and ______________.

✦ A good way to know if something has become an idol in your life is to ask yourself these questions:

1. Do I try hard to ______________ and will I think of creative ways to keep it?
2. Do I ______________ about the hold it has on me?
3. Do I ______________?

✦ God may want to do something ______________, but first He wants to do something ______________.

DAY 2

What Is My Real Issue?

After speaking for more than twenty years, I am not immune to speaking mishaps.

Several years ago, I had the unique experience of having to get up and walk to the stage to speak with a leg that had fallen asleep from sitting too long in a crossed position.

If you imagine my trek from seat to platform as being a bit like a newborn deer trying to find its legs, you are not far off. I was hesitant and a bit wobbly because the sensation of walking with a numb leg is weird. (My apologies to the audience in Colorado; I'm sure Gumby was not who you expected to speak to you that night!) Thankfully, I'm happy to report that despite my internal panic and extraordinarily slow and awkward gait, I made it to the stage that night without a face-plant.

You can probably relate to having a single limb go numb like this, but have you ever felt so numb and dead *inside* that it actually scared you? Maybe in that situation you thought, *Surely this numbness will wear off … I'll be better when I quit this something or do that something,* but your circumstances don't change anything, and you continue to experience the dullness of a life without joy or live in dread of the next day, no matter what.

Or maybe you suffer from the "shoulds": You *should* be happier because on the outside, you have everything. You *should* be closer to the Lord because you've been in church for a very long time. Still, inside you are numb.

We feel these emotions as part of being human—disappointment, fear, disillusionment, shame, even anger (yes, I named it, women). We get this way because life *gets to us* ... and then we wind up feeling desperate until we finally pay attention to the longing inside for more.

Parts of all these things were true for me in 2013, as the wife of a loving husband, a mom of growing kids with a dog and a house, living in comfortable suburbia, having just authored my next new book ... yet living with a deep dissatisfaction in my spiritual life. I was experiencing what I call the "sick-of-me life," where I was needing God to consume me more than my life currently was.

The sick-of-me life had me thinking and feeling these things:

- I am sick of being afraid.
- I am sick of being hot and cold for God, depending on my circumstance.
- I am sick of wrestling with the same things I've wrestled with for most of my life.
- I want to be well.
- I want to be productive and joyful.
- When I meet God one day, I want to say with open hands, "Here's what I did with the life You gave me."
- I want God. I want Him to show up tangibly in me. I want Him to blow me away with insights and remind me that He is bigger than all my daily crazy. I want Him to sweep me off my feet and take me on one of His many amazing adventures.

You know what it's like to want to jump out of your skin? That's what I felt like. My struggles might not have made sense to anyone on the outside. But only we and God know the true condition of our hearts. It wasn't that I didn't love or serve God. It's that I wanted (and needed) even *more* of Him.

So one day, after my kids went off to school, I got on the floor of my office, put my face in the carpet fibers, and prayed this prayer: "Okay, God, mess with me." This moment was, in every way, the cry of my own soul desperate to be revived.

I realize it was not a very fancy prayer. I have admittedly prayed better. But I needed God to help me. Even more: I longed for God—Himself. Praying the words "Okay, God, mess with me" was my way of saying, "I will not stop You from digging into any and every corner of my heart to do the work in me You need to do. The hidden parts. The hardest parts. The parts I don't even know need to be exposed. Just have Your way with all of them."

I did this because I was finally so sick of me that I was ready to seek Him. I wanted to come back to God. But even more than that: I wanted God. And I knew He could revive me.

I was ready to come alive.

What about you? Where are you right now?

Complete the following bar graph, filling the bar to show where you are for each of the following "places."

Place of Lack: A starving, desperate place where you need God to consume you more than what is currently consuming your life.

Place of Plenty: You have a lot, or it appears you do to others, but it's all surface, so it feels unsatisfying, and you want more for your life.

Place of Being Spiritually Dead: You don't feel close to God, or you feel as if you aren't growing but aren't sure how to change it.

Place of Searching: You feel as if something is missing from your life and you aren't sure what it is.

Lack	
Plenty	
Spiritually Dead	
Searching	

We can't move forward until we name where we are. Then revival is possible.

What does it mean to you to be revived?

Now look up the definition of *revival*.

Where do you want to go? Write down what you would like your spiritual life with the Lord to look like.

The real issue of coming to God or coming back to God is always a matter of the heart. But it's not just about the heart itself. We know that a half-hearted faith is not what God is looking for. He is looking for a person with an all-in heart.

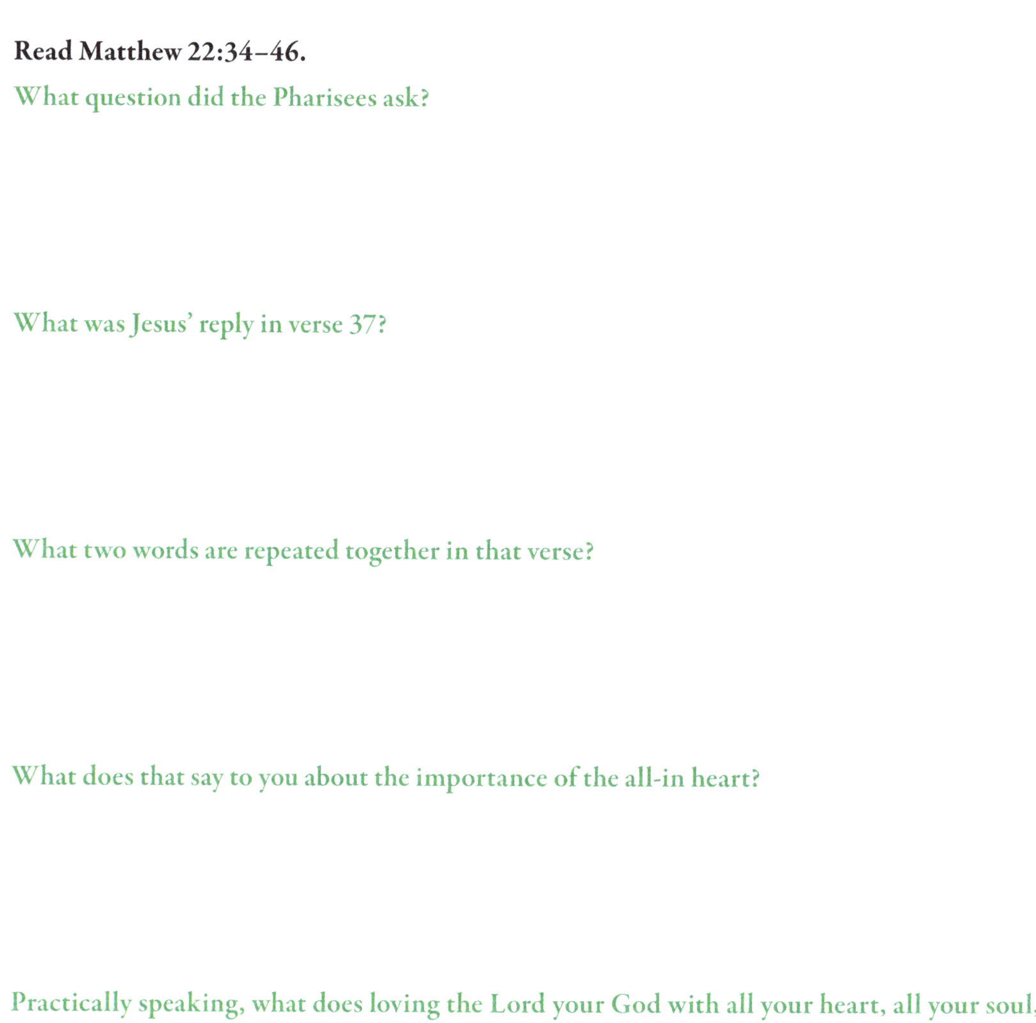

Read Matthew 22:34–46.

What question did the Pharisees ask?

What was Jesus' reply in verse 37?

What two words are repeated together in that verse?

What does that say to you about the importance of the all-in heart?

Practically speaking, what does loving the Lord your God with all your heart, all your soul, and all your mind look like on a Tuesday afternoon? When you are in a carpool line or at Target?

This is, to me, a matter of everyday character. It is allowing the Holy Spirit to control your words when you want to use words of your own that aren't kind to someone who cut you off in traffic. Or doing things that inconvenience you, like taking food to someone when you aren't gifted with hospitality because you long to please God more than yourself. Or seeking God in a moment when you could numb out to Netflix or indulge in a quicker, yet more temporary self-satisfier, like alcohol or overeating or shopping. Giving Him your whole heart is giving your adult child over to Him in full trust, even when he or she does not behave in ways that honor God. These things are ways you love God with your whole heart in everyday life.

What does Jeremiah 29:13 say is the result when you seek the Lord with your whole heart?

What does that suggest to you about the possibilities of revival (or being revived) when we come with an all-in heart?

See, friend, the real issue for revival is this:

1. **We must acknowledge where we are and pray for the desire to go where God wants to take us.** (We just looked at where we are as we started this study.)
2. **We must not only know we *need* God, but we must *want* God.** (We will talk about this much more tomorrow!)
3. **Wanting God is a desire of the *all-in* heart.** David wrote Psalm 142 while in the cave of Adullam, being pursued and persecuted by Saul, and these words in verse 5 are especially compelling in the context of singular desire: "Then I pray to you, O LORD. I say, 'You are my place of refuge. You are all I really want in life.'" Not only did David know that God was his ultimate place of safety and rest; he also desired nothing but Him, even in the moment he was facing imminent death. David's heart wanted the right thing, which brought him not only the right perspective but also peace.

4. Revival comes when we want God with our whole hearts.

You might be thinking, *This sounds amazing. I want this. But how do I get an all-in heart?* I'm so glad you asked. I will help you with that the rest of this week.

But to close out today, let's start with a few Revival Resets to begin shifting our perspectives.

Remember: Revival starts with acknowledging where we are and praying for the desire to go where God wants to take us.

Write out your personal revival resets to add to this list or a prayer for personal revival as we go into day 3.

REVIVAL RESETS

I'm Tired of ...	I Want to ...
fighting for people to love me.	fight for people to love God.
this chase for approval.	be revived to pursue only an audience of One.
watching other people serve God.	partner with God for the kingdom rather than sit on the sidelines!
being halfway in with God.	get off the spiritual roller coaster and make progress.
making decisions based on my fear of the unknown and my desire for comfort.	be free from the chains that have kept me bound.
trying to control everything.	finally know and rest in God's ability to take care of it all.

I'm Tired of ...	I Want to ...

DAY 3

What Do I Want?

One of my favorite stories is in John 1:35–38. For a bit of context, John the Baptist, a hairy guy who ate bugs (and the Bible doesn't say this, but I guarantee he smelled), had been going around preaching about Christ and His coming. This was yet another day he was preaching about the coming of Jesus, and because of John's uniqueness, people wondered if the coming Messiah he preached about might even be him, but John was always quick to defer to Jesus, the one he loved.

> The following day John was again standing with two of his disciples. As Jesus walked by, John looked at him and declared, "Look! There is the Lamb of God!" When John's two disciples heard this, they followed Jesus.
>
> Jesus looked around and saw them following. "What do you want?" he asked them.

Out of all the questions Jesus could have asked, why do you think He chose "What do you want?"

When you read Jesus' question "What do you want?" I don't want you to hear it like that of a child asking a parent for something and the parent responding in a huff of frustration ("What do you want?!"). In the first English translation of the Bible it read "What seek ye?"—in other words, "What are you looking for?"—a question of great intention and purpose, like all questions Jesus asked in the Bible.

Look up and write down Matthew 6:33.

What are we supposed to seek first?

> "As with the verb 'to follow,' so also with Jesus' question, *What do you want?* It appears that the Evangelist is writing on two levels. The question makes sense as straightforward narrative: Jesus asks the two men who are following him to articulate what is on their minds. But the Evangelist wants his readers to reflect on a deeper question: the Logos-Messiah confronts those who make any show of beginning to follow him and demands that they articulate what they really want in life."[1]

The question "What do you want?" is, in my view, the most important question Jesus ever asked because in it is the crux of all life. What we want drives what we do. What we fight for. What we tolerate. What we chase. What we love. Jesus knew what these disciples wanted, because our sovereign Lord knows all. The question wasn't for Him but for *them*. He wanted *them* to know for themselves what they were looking for. And most important, He wanted to get to the heart of which kingdom they were seeking: His or theirs. This would determine what they would choose, how they would live, and, yes, how they would die in the end—something He knew but they would only come to fully realize.

Why do you think Jesus did *not* ask the question "What do you *need*?"

It would be reasonable to think that Jesus might ask about these men's needs. But He did not do that in John 1. Is it because He already knew their needs? Maybe, but He also already knew their wants, and He still asked them about that. (He knows any answer to any question He might ask. Jesus intentionally asked every question recorded; He did not misspeak or flippantly ask them. So every question holds great importance.)

You might assume, at first, that Jesus asked about wants versus needs to get these men to recognize their selfishness or to call out secret sin. After all, asking about what they wanted could expose their wrong desires. Perhaps this is true, in part, for us too, as we take personal inventory of where we are off mission; our desire for God is always key in the topic of what we chase and how we feed our carnal cravings.

But don't assume this automatically means that Jesus was downplaying or chastising desire itself. In fact, He knows how very important it is—so much so that He addressed it instead of need because He knew need was not enough. It simply isn't a strong enough motivator. And though we were created with needs, we were also created with the physiology to desire. It is in our very nature, or we would be unfeeling, unmoved, unable to be drawn into longing or craving.

Look up Psalm 37:4. What does the first part of this verse say is the key to the last part (about desire)?

> "Thou hast formed us for Thyself, and our hearts are restless till they find rest in Thee."[2]

Not only is God not opposed to desire, but He endorses it. The issue of desire, though, is to center on Him. This is where we typically go wrong.

As desire is the key to the rest of how we live our lives—**our daily lives will reflect what and who we desire**—if we desire God, we will live for His kingdom, doing eternally focused things. If, though, we desire the world, we will live for the world, doing worldly, now-focused things. This is a simple human equation that looks like this:

Desire → Eternal or Temporal Focus = Daily Lifestyle

Practically, an eternal focus as a lifestyle:

- We desire God more than anything, so we choose a man or woman to marry who also desires God above all.
- We desire God more than anything, so we are compelled by the gospel to serve others, even when it doesn't come naturally to us.
- We desire God more than anything, so we are willing to sit in uncomfortable conversations in order to make amends with people we have hurt or feel hurt by.

These are just a few examples.

Write out a practical example of what a "now" (temporal) focused life could look like:

But for a lot of Christians there is a disconnect and, as a result, a major problem.

In the quest to "do the right thing," "please God," and "make Him happy," we have decided we should not address our desires. We have come to believe, either by direct teaching or by assumption, that desire itself is a taboo subject. That our lives are solely to be about meeting the needs of other people. That the biblical way of dying to self means denying desire.

So we ask, "What do other people need?" And we have become chronic people-pleasers, misunderstanding what it means to serve biblically.

Look up Galatians 5:13.

What has God called us to live in?

How are we supposed to serve one another?

Why is serving people with the wrong motive of people-pleasing not doing it in the true freedom of service God has called us to?

Interestingly, when we finally become burned out from all our scrambling to meet others' needs from a place of people-pleasing rather than true biblical service, we ask ourselves, "What do I need?" And we then decide what we need is a vacation, a new job, or to rest. This usually happens when we are in a place of burnout.

But you cannot revive the deep needs of your soul with a five-day vacation.

On a scale of 1 to 10, how often do you consider the needs of others?

On a scale of 1 to 10, how often do you consider your own needs?

What do you think dying to self means according to Luke 9:23?

Have you ever thought dying to self means denying desire? Why or why not?

> You cannot revive the deep needs of your soul with a five-day vacation.

The truth is, when we deny desire, we cut off a created part of our spiritual life—the components of desire: vulnerability, trust, love, passion. Yes, many times we have misdirected desires, but that comes from how we feed our desire component, not from desire itself being wrong!

With so many of us cutting off these important components for desire, it is no wonder we live our lives with a lost spiritual connection!

How has cutting off a created part of yourself—these components of desire—caused you to lose spiritual connection, if it has?

Recently, I asked a group of ministry leaders that I coach, "What do you want?" None of them could answer me. At first, this might seem like no big deal. But when you consider the many recent public falls in leadership, I think it's worth considering. (You might be thinking, "Didn't they do exactly what they wanted, which is what got them in trouble?" Keep reading and I'll explain more of what I think happens.)

As I mentioned before, many Christians assume we are holier or more noble if we spend our time addressing the needs of people and neglecting all our own wants. It feels selfish, especially as we serve folks with great needs. (And yes, we live in a self-centered culture. But addressing desire isn't the same as living self-indulgently, just as serving others isn't the same as people-pleasing.)

God wants us to want Him. We need desire and other feelings in order to do that. So our mindset needs to change, to understand the importance of desire and the true motive in serving others.

When we do not honor desire, we wind up doing two things:

1. We *express it* negatively by acting out in misplaced ways (liberalism/overindulgence/misdirection). This is what has happened in many public ministry falls, marital affairs, etc.
2. We *suppress it,* and it comes out in negative ways (legalism, fundamentalism, judgmentalism). This mindset can make us very judgmental of others, rigid in our own faith, and eventually may cause us to deconstruct or act out when we ourselves are hurt by it.

Both result in an eventual crash and burn.

Describe what you understand this "crash and burn" to be. Have you ever had a time when you expressed your desires negatively or suppressed your desires because you thought they were wrong (and had the wrong idea about them at their core)? Write about that and the ramifications.

No, needs are not enough. Wants drive us. And I believe Jesus addressed desire in John 1 so the men would do three things:

1. Understand that the kingdom of God is what they were supposed to be seeking, first and foremost.
2. Consider if they were desiring the right thing(s) (always, ultimately Him).
3. Assess the consequences of their focus, now and in the future.

This is the same process of consideration for us today.

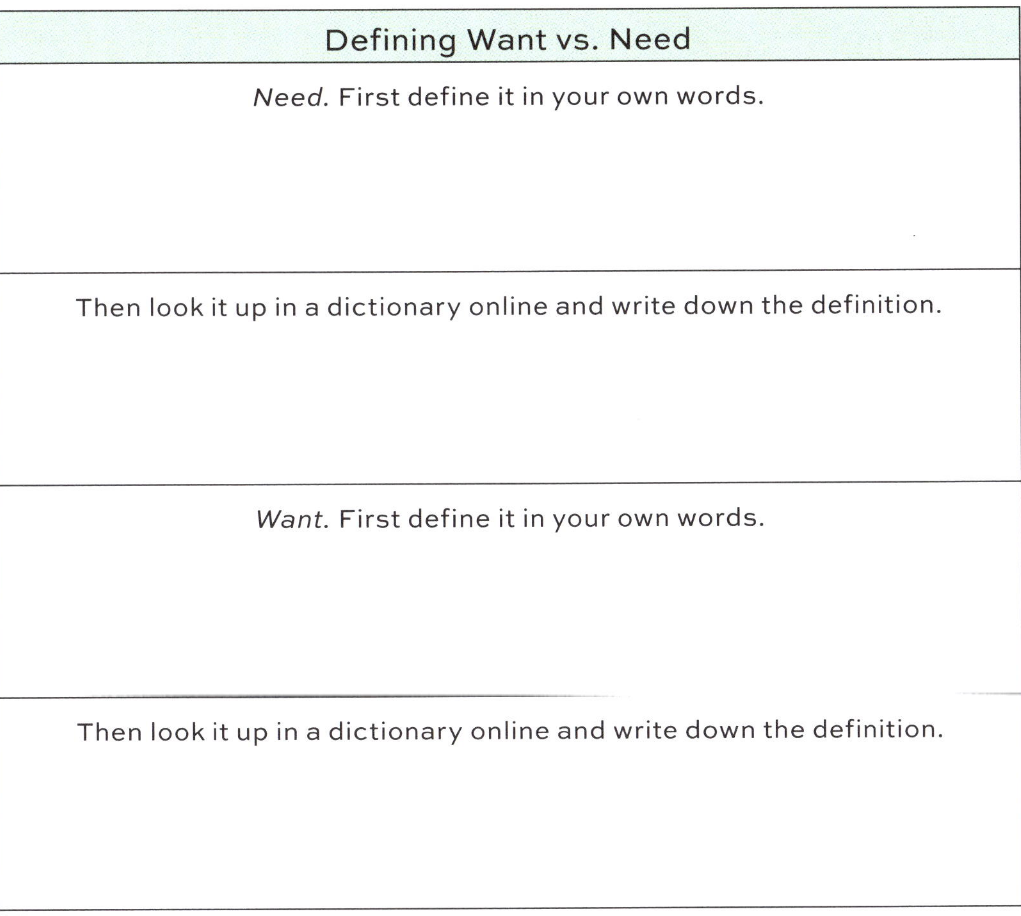

Defining Want vs. Need
Need. First define it in your own words.
Then look it up in a dictionary online and write down the definition.
Want. First define it in your own words.
Then look it up in a dictionary online and write down the definition.

To want something is to have a strong desire or wish for it. Wants can be physical, emotional, or intellectual. For example, you might want to eat a delicious meal, to be loved and accepted, or to learn a new skill. Wants are different from needs. Needs—such as food, water, and shelter—are essential for survival. Wants are not essential for survival, but they make our lives fulfilling. Wants are also different from wishes. (Wishes are often for things that are unattainable or unlikely to happen.) Wants are more realistic and achievable.

In my own life, there have been many times I have *needed* to mend a relationship with someone, but I have not *wanted* to pick up the phone to call that person to make things right.

I have *needed* to get healthier, but I have not *wanted* to do the work of moving my body more or having better nutrition to treat my body better.

I have *needed* to have a stronger relationship with the Lord, but I have not *wanted* to focus on the daily disciplines of prayer and reading my Bible—instead I have wanted to look at my phone in the morning more than I have wanted to feast on God's Word.

List three things you know you need to do right now on a small to a large scale—can be either! (For example: I need to get healthy, I need to clean my house, I need to mend a relationship with a friend, etc.)

1. I need to ____.

2. I need to ____.

3. I need to ____.

Now complete each sentence by noting why you honestly don't do those things.

1. But I don't want to ______________________________________.

2. But I don't want to ______________________________________.

3. But I don't want to ______________________________________.

There is no doubt that we need God. You can probably list fifty ways you need God right now. However, if you want to have a soul revival and truly follow Him, you have to want Him and want Him *most.* (More on this tomorrow.)

Reread John 1:35–38.

Now imagine Jesus turning to you and asking, "What do you want?" How would you answer that? (Be honest. He already knows.)

Now let's think about this in the context of revival.

Recall your first encounter with Jesus. Describe how you "wanted" Him in that moment.

Think of where you are presently. How has your "want" changed?

Over time, our tendency is to become numb and stale to the things of the Lord and to the Lord Himself. This happens for a number of reasons, least of which is because we *want* it to happen. Most of us don't intend to become stale Christians. But it happens before we know it.

Let's personalize this a bit. If you read my book *Jesus over Everything*, you know I went on a one-year shopping fast. But I certainly didn't ever think I would need to detox from shopping. I never intended to become an overindulger in my shopping habits. After all, I am not an extravagant person. I do not buy expensive things. At the time the Lord convicted me of my shopping idol, I did not even own a credit card.

> "Our moving away from God blinds our eyes to the things He is doing. Our minds feel entitled to the things He will do. Our hearts are calloused to the things He has already done."[3]

There were several revealing moments spanning multiple years that led to me admitting my shopping habits were really meant to numb a feeling or delay facing a reality or even having a conversation with God. Sometimes I didn't want to talk to the Lord, and shopping gave me something else to do. Sometimes I wanted to feel better about my relationship with my body, and shopping helped fix that for a minute with a cute shirt. It's not that buying a cute shirt was wrong; it was that buying a cute shirt was never enough. So I had to keep buying one more. Before I knew it, I had a closetful of cute shirts and a bad habit of running to buy another every time I wanted an emotional fix.

One time, I went to a darling boutique to innocently buy one outfit for a speaking event in a tropical location. After all, the Lord would surely speak through me a bit more powerfully if I matched the aesthetic, I mentally reasoned. *Before I knew it,* I had an armful of clothes to take to the dressing room. *Before I knew it,* I was trying on more clothes I hadn't come to buy. *Before I knew it,* I was lugging those clothes to the register and watching the woman ring them up, without saying a word of protest or denial. *Before I knew it,* I was spending a lot of money—much more than I ever intended. I had come in for one outfit, but I went out with much more.

Have you ever had a "before I knew it" time in your life, when you never intended to become numb to something but over time your habits desensitized you to it? Write about it.

Sometimes we become numb to the things of the Lord because we are such blessed people. (Yes, you read that right.) Our inability to deal with disappointment exposes our level of entitlement resulting from the gifts God has given us. We attach God's goodness to how well things are going. We take things for granted every day. Especially here in the Western world, we do not understand what it is like to be in want, so desire centers around *excess*. Were we to develop gratitude, we would often want the better, kingdom things. (Doubt what I'm saying? Think about how increasingly hard it has become for kids to even come up with a Christmas list anymore. They have so much they don't know what to want for!)

It is important to be honest about this with ourselves—and with God. Yesterday, when we took inventory of where we were, it was a vital step. Telling ourselves the truth is critical. Stay tuned for day 5 of this week, when I'll help you see how to stir the soul revival you need.

So, what can help us not grow numb to God?

I want us to think about the idea of spiritual *rootedness*. As we plant deep in Christ, it results in an ongoing revived spirit. Many of us struggle with temporary desire and the need for quick highs of experiential faith because we do not allow our faith to become rooted by the practice of spiritual disciplines, day after day, year after year.

Evaluating what we want needs to be in the context of what we want for the long haul, the duration, the future—not just for right now. It is not about feelings in the moment. It is about deep-rooted faith—the kind that must be established and cultivated over time. I highly encourage you to see your wants in that light. More immediate wants are not wrong; they just do not compare to the deeper things, like longevity, growth, and holiness. I love this verse for that reason:

> Let your roots grow down into him, and let your lives be built on him. Then your faith will grow strong in the truth you were taught, and you will overflow with thankfulness. (Col. 2:7)

This tree represents the wants you have—what you are currently looking for in your life. Write on the branches the more surface wants (again, not wrong—just different). Write on the roots the deeper wants. They can be spiritual or material; God knows and cares about them all.

DAY 4

What Is in My Way?

What is keeping you from wanting God most? This is an important question.

I told you about my past shopping habit, which on the surface might seem like a silly, harmless pastime—one most women love and that wouldn't possibly keep me from wanting God most.

The problem is, it did distract me from God. Because *anything* can. Yes, even "harmless" things, like shopping. Anything we run to in moments when we could run to the Lord can become idols. Anything we learn to lean on for comfort. Anything that temporarily fills the hole meant only for the love of Christ.

I know it's a tough concept because, truly, shopping is not a sin. But it becomes a matter of what we want most: a deeper connection with the Lord or to cling to the habit that is in the way of that.

> "I've learned that the best way to end something is to let it starve. You just stop feeding it. Then you know if it really has power over you." (Anonymous)

When I was in the midst of trying to determine if shopping really had become an issue for me, I posed these questions to myself: *What if some dumb clothes—my habit of running to buy them to make me feel better—are in fact coming between me and the God I need and long to hear from the most? Am I then robbing myself of what I actually want ... working against myself in a way?*

There was only one way to test the theory. I needed to take a break from my shopping habit to make room to hear from the Lord. And pretty soon, I knew the answer to my question. My shopping had in fact been in the way of my relationship with Him. The less time and attention I gave to my shopping, the more time and attention I had for the Lord. In return, I heard Him speaking to me more, and this brought us closer in our relationship. It was a simple shift in focus to Him, but one that changed everything.

We tend to get frustrated when we don't hear from God or we don't feel close to Him. We may think it's His fault, or we may know it's us but we don't know how to "fix" the relationship. So our natural next step is to attempt to do more spiritual things. We volunteer more at church. We barter with God or promise Him big things. But what if it's not about doing more but instead, it's about changing some of our current habits?

What are some ways you've attempted to feel close to God that have made sense in the moment but proven futile or at least frustrating in the end?

As Pascal once famously said, "What else does this craving, and this helplessness, proclaim but that there was once in man a true happiness, of which all that now remains is the empty print and trace? This he tries in vain to fill with everything around him, seeking in things that are not there the help he cannot find in those that are, though none can help, since this infinite abyss can be filled only with an infinite and immutable object; in other words by God himself."[1]

These can be good and worthy efforts. Serving the church is wonderful, fasting is a spiritual discipline, and the Bible talks about fleeing temptation. But behavior modification alone is not what brings us closer to the Lord.

What if I told you that what keeps you from your desire for God and the revival you want is that your craving for Him is being temporarily satisfied with something that attempts to mimic the real thing ... which never allows you to fully feel the emptiness inside you that longs for God?

Bottom line: You are letting idols get in the way of revival.

Read Joshua 24. Backstory: Old and about to die in Joshua 23, Joshua has just given his farewell speech to the Israelites and, at the same time, given some exhortative commands, like "Be strong and courageous." Now in Joshua 24 he has summoned tribe leaders, judges, and officers and strongly reminded them not only of what they have seen with their own eyes of the Lord's deliverance and goodness but also of their own waywardness when they knew better. He calls out their idolatry and bids them to choose.

The interchange that happens between Joshua and the Israelites in verses 14–23 is so crucial that I am dropping it in here:

> "So fear the LORD and serve him wholeheartedly. Put away forever the idols your ancestors worshiped when they lived beyond the Euphrates River and in Egypt. Serve the LORD alone. But if you refuse to serve the LORD, then choose today whom you will serve. Would you prefer the gods your ancestors served beyond the Euphrates? Or will it be the gods of the Amorites in whose land you now live? But as for me and my family, we will serve the LORD."
>
> The people replied, "We would never abandon the LORD and serve other gods. For the LORD our God is the one who rescued us and our ancestors from slavery in the land of Egypt. He performed mighty miracles before our very eyes. As we traveled through the wilderness among our enemies, he preserved us. It was the LORD who drove out the Amorites and the other nations living here in the land. So we, too, will serve the LORD, for he alone is our God."
>
> Then Joshua warned the people, "You are not able to serve the LORD, for he is a holy and jealous God. He will not forgive your rebellion and your sins. If you abandon the LORD and serve other gods, he will turn against you and destroy you, even though he has been so good to you."
>
> But the people answered Joshua, "No, we will serve the LORD!"
>
> "You are a witness to your own decision," Joshua said. "You have chosen to serve the LORD."
>
> "Yes," they replied, "we are witnesses to what we have said."

> "All right then," Joshua said, "destroy the idols among you, and turn your hearts to the LORD, the God of Israel."

There's so much happening here that I don't want you to miss. **Take a minute to notice the progression in this conversation and coinciding verses, and circle the words showing it.**

Let's recap:

1. Joshua calls out the idolatry in their lives (v. 14).
2. Joshua tells them to choose between the idols and God (v. 15).
3. The people are in denial over their idols (vv. 16–18).
4. Joshua reprimands them for their denial and repeats the truth to them (v. 19–20).
5. The people are adamant that they choose God (v. 21).
6. Joshua tells them exactly what to do to please God: destroy the idols and turn their hearts to God (v. 23).

Let's break this down a bit.

What does this passage mean to you, in a modern context, and what can we learn from the Israelites in this moment?

So many of us have likely read this verse: "Choose today whom you will serve ... As for me and my family, we will serve the LORD," but I doubt most of us have known that this verse was in a passage about idolatry.

First, define *idolatry* in your own words.

Now, look up *idolatry*, ideally in a biblical commentary or the Logos Bible study app or (last option) Google.

Late pastor and author Timothy Keller describes an idol like this: "It's whatever you look at and say, in your heart of hearts, 'If I have that, then I'll feel my life has meaning, then I'll know I have value, then I'll feel significant and secure.' There are many ways to describe that kind of relationship to something, but perhaps the best one is *worship*."[2]

> What keeps you from your desire for God and the revival you want is that your craving for Him is being temporarily satisfied with something that attempts to mimic the real thing ... which never allows you to fully feel the emptiness inside you that longs for God.

But idols can also be sneakier than that. They can be unintentional objects of our affection. Ways we spend our time and money that do not overtly tell us, *I am overtaking you. I am giving you meaning, taking the place of God in your life.* It's true that an idol is anything more important to you than God, anything that absorbs your heart and imagination more than God does, anything you seek to give you what only God can give. But it doesn't always look that way.

My idol was shopping, but from the outside you would never have known it. I bought things for a bargain. I wasn't in credit card debt. I never lived beyond my means. Yet my habit of buying clothes and home décor items in moments of boredom or sadness or to escape some feeling rather than take it to the Lord went from innocent to ensnaring in a matter of a few years.

Before long, my closet was brimming over. My home had more pillows than any couch could hold. I was hiding purchases from my husband. I was feeling the Lord's conviction to deal with the real issue rather than head to the store and swipe my debit card once again.

For months, I ignored it. Until finally, through a series of events (which I write about in my book *Jesus over Everything*), I confessed my idol. There was only one way to know if my shopping had gotten in the way of the relationship with the Lord I was seeking in my life—the revival my soul needed ... I decided to lay down shopping for a time and see if, indeed, it had become an idol. I soon found out it had. The peace and joy I felt after taking a break from shopping was a large sign. The freedom even in the obedience to lay it down was my first clue. And the depth of friendship it brought the Lord and me in the months of growing closeness changed my life forever.

Is there something you sense the Lord may be asking you to lay down for a time to see if it has become an idol? Name it without trying to excuse it or talk yourself out of it.

What would need to change in your life if God revealed to you that was an idol?

Write out a plan for breaking from (not doing the behavior of) your idol for a time in this chart. Include the specific behaviors you feel led to set aside, the length of time you'll fast from each, who your accountability partner(s) will be, better ways to replace that behavior, and Scriptures to dwell on.

Behaviors	
Length	
Accountability Partner(s)	
Better Ways	
Scriptures	

I did not set out to fast for a whole year from shopping. I meant to do it for six weeks, but after that time the Lord said to me, "You're not done." So we kept going. It was a beautiful and, especially at first, difficult detox. But by God's grace, I was able to put what had become my idol aside; it was getting in the way of my desire for God and by virtue of that, the revival my soul desperately craved. New clothes could not fill my heart. They could not provide comfort in my grief. That substitute savior was not unlike the Israelites' idolatry back in Joshua's day. I had to choose between my idol and God. When you think about it that way, what a silly choice to ever pick a habit like shopping over God, the great Lover of my soul.

But that's what idols do: they fool you into thinking you aren't worshipping them.

Over the next five sessions we will explore different idols. I don't know what it will be for you specifically, but I do know that we all have them.

Before we move on, I want to leave you with one thing I hope will be helpful to you. You may be asking, How do I know if something has become an idol in my life? It's a fair and common question, because sometimes it's hard to distinguish between what is just a harmless habit and what is a more stubborn idol that is truly causing us harm.

Here are the questions I would ask myself:

1. Does the thought of parting with ______ make me sad or anxious?
2. Do I try to hide how much ______ is part of my life?
3. Am I plotting ways to keep ______ in my life?

Try asking yourself these questions about each of your suspect behaviors. If you answer yes to any, it has likely become an idol.

DAY 5

How Can I Have a Soul Revival?

Jesus' question "Do you want to be well?" which he asked the sick man at the pool of Bethesda in John 5, often compels me. It is yet another incredible question the Lord asks that He already knows the answer to but asks anyway.

This question, I believe, was asked of the sick man not only to reveal his own narrative (which we know because in the next verse he says, "I can't" and explains his plight) but also to let him know he can't get well without Jesus.

The truth is, we look for lots of ways to heal ourselves and stir up our souls spiritually, but without the Lord, we cannot conjure up wellness or lasting fulfillment. This is where the issue of what we want comes in. Do we truly want God? And even more: Do we want Him more than anything else?

I teach something very important in *I Want God* called the principle of the greater desire,[1] which is: you are willing to forgo what you want in the moment for what you want more. Most of us do not know how to tell ourselves no ... about anything. Deferring is an abstract concept to a please-me-now culture. But the life of a believer in Jesus is all about the life of the greater desire, which says, "I want to be well and whole more than I want to be tied to something that brings me down. I want to be alive in spirit more than I want to just make it through the day.

I want God to consume me more than the mess that is currently consuming my life." It is saying, ultimately: "I want God more than I want my idols."

If Jesus were asking us today if we wanted to be well, operating in the principle of the greater desire, we would say, "Yes, and because of that, I'll give up my idol of _________." If He were asking the question from John 1, "What do you want?" and we were operating in the principle of the greater desire, we would say, "I want You, God, and I want You more than __________."

> Afterward Jesus returned to Jerusalem for one of the Jewish holy days. Inside the city, near the Sheep Gate, was the pool of Bethesda, with five covered porches. Crowds of sick people—blind, lame, or paralyzed—lay on the porches. One of the men lying there had been sick for thirty-eight years. When Jesus saw him and knew he had been ill for a long time, he asked him, "Would you like to get well?"
>
> "I can't, sir," the sick man said, "for I have no one to put me into the pool when the water bubbles up. Someone else always gets there ahead of me." (John 5:1–7)

Using this example, give your own answers (operating in the principle of the greater desire):

To Jesus' question "Do you want to be well?" ______________________________

To Jesus' question "What do you want?" ______________________________

A powerful way to want God is to meditate on the Scripture. I especially love the longings of the psalmists—the raw and poignant expressions of unabashed desire for the Lord. As we read their passion and love, it draws our own hearts in.

Look up each of these short passages from Psalms and write them down.
Psalm 73:25–26

Psalm 27:4

Psalm 42:1–2

Psalm 63:1–2

Psalm 142:5

Now write your own expression of desire for the Lord:

When I told my father, a longtime pastor, that I was writing about revival some years ago (I first released *I Want God* in 2014), something powerful came over his face as he clearly went back to a profound memory. "Lisagirl," he said (this was his nickname for me), "I preached on revival once, and maybe you'd like to hear about it." Instead of a pulpit, he grabbed the sides of his living room chair, muting the ball game on the TV and speaking into the wood-paneled room as if he were in front of a listening church congregation. It profoundly impacted me that night and has stuck with me ever since. It's a beautiful model of how to experience ongoing soul revival, straight from the book of Revelation.[2]

The three important parts of a soul revival:

1. Remember
2. Repent
3. Repeat

"The author of Revelation identifies himself as John, a servant of God and spiritual brother to the members of the seven churches (1:1, 4, 9; 22:8). John is further designated as a prophet (22:6, 9) who was residing on the island of Patmos in the eastern Aegean Sea, 'because of the word of God and the testimony of Jesus' (1:9 NASB). Likely, his presence on Patmos was not for the purpose of proclaiming the word of God, but rather he had been exiled there as punishment by the state for preaching."[3]

Read Revelation 2:2–5. John, the writer of Revelation, had received a vision from God for the seven churches in Asia—and for Christians everywhere. The result is the book of Revelation, and the first part of chapter 2 was written to the church at Ephesus. Ephesus was one of the most influential cities in the eastern part of the Roman Empire, and Paul had ministered here for three years. He had told the church that false teachers would come and try to lead them away from the faith. And that is exactly what happened.

Reread verses 2–3. What kind of people made up the Ephesian church? Write down all the qualities you can mine here.

God established early on that these were good people. Good churchgoing, service-loving people. They were doing the most. That wasn't the problem. In case we need to remember that our good deeds aren't what God is after, let us remember the Ephesian church.

Reread verse 4. What is the Lord after? (Hint: It's in the complaint.)

It's important to note that in this verse (v. 4), the church at Ephesus has *left* their first love, not *lost* their first love. Often, we think (scratch that: *feel*) God leaves us, but the truth is, we leave Him. Leaving is deliberate, even if the leaving is drifting; if I leave something, someone, or someplace, I can always go back. I know where I left it. If I lose something, I often have no idea where it is, as losing is often accidental. The church at Ephesus left God out of their own willfulness, not out of helplessness. Carelessness may have played a part, but they still made the choices that eventually led them to drift away.

Take a minute to consider your distance from God in this moment or any past moments of your life. Think of it in the context of having left Him versus having lost Him. In what way(s) did you leave Him, and how does thinking about it like that make a difference with you?

Leaving Him vs.	Losing Him

Practicing Soul Revival

One of the things I love most about God is that He does not expose a problem without providing a solution. The ultimate problem/solution is, of course, sin and death with new life and resurrection through His death for us on the cross, and in every lesser way as He shows us how to course correct in the Bible. Even as He tells the Ephesian church the complaint He has against them, He tells them how to atone for it:

REMEMBER—THE FIRST STEP

Write down Revelation 2:4–5a.

What is the phrase in verse 5a that stands out?

"Look how far you have fallen" suggests there is a big gap between where the Ephesians once were with God and where they are now. That gap represents one thing: forgetfulness.

My friend, author Michele Cushatt, has a powerful quote in her book *Undone*: "How quickly one miracle is forgotten when another one is wanted."[4] We are a forgetful people who often take the power, character, benefits, and miracles of God for granted.

It's one of the reasons I love the whole book of Deuteronomy so much, but especially chapters 29–30, where Moses gives his famous last speech to the Israelites. In it, he calls the people to remembrance. He knows that helping them remember before they go live a life of ease and plenty in the Promised Land is key—it is then they will be at risk because they will be comfortable. And in their comfort they will be like all of us in a less needy state: less likely to call on God.

Remember a time in your life when you felt helpless and most needy of God. Write down the details. Were you at a comfortable place in your life or at a place of personal grief, lack, or crisis?

What was God's response?

We think we are most at risk of losing everything when we are in crisis, but the truth is we are at the most risk when we are not in crisis. It is then when we forget about God.

But as we remember God, we want God more. And that desire leads to greater and greater passion.

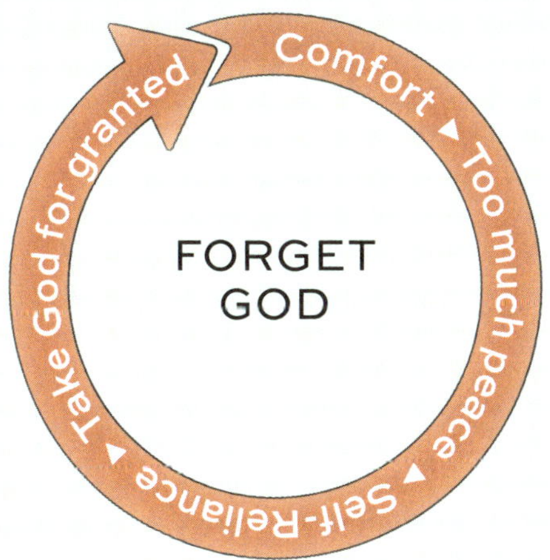

REPENT—THE SECOND STEP

I used to be averse to the word *repent*. It reminded me of fiery, sweaty preachers telling us we were all going to hell in a handbasket if we didn't repent! What I didn't realize was that *repentance* is a serious word but not a scary word. It's a beautiful word, actually. It's our way back to the Lord when we have moved away from Him.

Write down your definition of the word *repentance*.

Now look up the word, preferably at the Logos Bible study app or something similar, but (last resort) you can look on Google. Write down any differences you find between this definition and your own.

Think about your idol(s). Remember what we read in Joshua 24. God takes idolatry seriously. If we've put anything before Him, we need to repent for that, come clean, and make things right with Him. The Ephesian church certainly had need of repentance.

Read Revelation 2:5 again. What does the phrase "Turn back to me" mean to you?

Repentance is a decision, not a feeling. That may be what we've gotten wrong. Where we have chosen to turn away ("Turn back to me" suggests there has been a turning-away point), we choose to course correct. It is an about-face, where our feelings may often follow our actions. This is a decision that honors the Lord. It is why we follow the Lord, despite our fleshly desires. And in so doing, we stoke revival in our soul.

REPEAT—THE THIRD STEP

We are a people who try hard at first—in our marriages, at our jobs, with our neighbors. (We bring new neighbors brownies, and we don't even bake!) We just love making good first impressions, even if they aren't completely accurate.

But God doesn't want us to try to impress Him. He doesn't want our good behavior for the sake of good behavior either. He made that clear to the good Ephesian church.

Read verse 5b one more time. Notice the last phrase, "do the works you did at first."

I find it interesting that the Lord spent two whole verses complimenting the Ephesians by naming all the good things they were doing. He did not miss a thing. He named each good deed, one by one. It was as if He wanted to clearly point out everything, so they would know He had seen it, so they would not worry that it was not noted and be tempted to point it out.

Why do you think it's significant that the Lord complimented the good work and character of the Ephesians, particularly in light of this phrase in verse 5?

If you answered that He wanted them to know that the "works" He was talking about were the inward works, not the physical works, I believe you're right. It wasn't about doing more. It was about *being* more. Becoming more like Him. This is the thing that will bring our souls revival and bring the world more of Jesus.

Perhaps you would say to me that you already read your Bible, already pray, already serve the Lord. I would say to you that this is wonderful. But I would also say to you, according to Revelation 2, to keep doing it. And do it again and again. And again. Repeat those spiritual disciplines to ignite those passions for God and keep them ignited.

Remember: Repeating is not a onetime magic moment. It is a daily, inward seeking. It is repeated heart and soul and mind work. It is an inside job.

Reflect on your week. How might you remember, repent, and repeat this week?

Remember	Repent	Repeat

Session 2

MORE THAN COMFORT

GOD IS KIND, BUT HE'S NOT SOFT.
IN KINDNESS HE TAKES US FIRMLY
BY THE HAND AND LEADS US
INTO A RADICAL LIFE-CHANGE.

Romans 2:4 (MSG)

Memorize this verse this week by our repetition model.

To follow along in the *I Want God* book, read chapters 4–5.

DAY 1

Video and Outline

Stream the "More Than Comfort" (session 2) video (link on p. 17) and complete the session 2 outline below as you watch.

Group leaders: See the session 2 guide in the back (p. 191) for group discussion information.

- **The idol of ____________________ might be what is stopping you from experiencing lasting, deep, and true revival.**
- **Everything has a ____________. We just don't always think about that at the time we are enjoying a temporary solution.**
- **Comfort in and of itself is not an idol. ________________________ is our great comforter, and He desires that we bring ________________________ to Him so He can properly comfort us.**
- **We turn comfort into an idol when we ____________________. The problem comes in when we try to comfort ourselves through ________________________ _______________ instead of Christ.**

✦ Comfort presents like the best friend you will ever have, but in the process of "comforting" you, it ______ what you really want in ______ right out from under you.

✦ What comfort really does to you:

- It affects your relationships with ______.
- It affects your relationship with ______.
- It affects your relationship with ______.

✦ When God allows ______ in our lives, He does us the biggest favor we never wanted.

✦ Taking comfort into our own hands gets in our way because it keeps us from:

1. Knowing ______.
2. Living in ______ with a healthy ______.
3. Enjoying our full ______ ______.

✦ God will always be the ______ and ______ comfort we need in the midst of this difficult life.

✦ As you seek to have revival in this area of your life and come back to God, ______ who He is as the great comforter, ______ from that comfort idol that's gotten in your way, and ______ that continual seeking of Him to bring you what you need to soothe and relieve your weary soul.

DAY 2

What Is My Real Issue?

I learned early on, quite subliminally, that when I was feeling angst about something, food could be my comfort.

Have a long, hard day at school? It's nothing two crunchy tacos from Taco Bell can't fix. Getting a filling at the dentist? Get a milkshake at McDonald's to forget all about it. I wasn't raised in the age of calorie consciousness, so Little Debbie cakes were not forbidden in my house. I loved that my mom did not focus heavily on food, one way or the other. Candidly, we just lived in a different time of health consciousness, so I forbid you to judge her. It wasn't until college that I even became aware that I should move my body any more than normal walking to and fro, and that eating when you were either sad or happy *just to eat* wasn't a great idea. People just weren't talking about that.

I'm sure a lot of us can relate to food being a central part of our lives. And for good reason: food, created by God for nourishment of our bodies, which He created, is *good*. No one in my family needed to teach me to eat when I was sad or feel shame when I took in sugary calories. Our human instinct pulls us to idolize whatever it can, even good things, to comfort us.

As I grew up, reaching for food to comfort me became more instinctual. I wanted food, and I felt I needed it. Because I had trained my feelings to desire food, my mind actually believed it needed food in moments I wasn't even physically hungry. Thus, my dependence on food to comfort me grew—a short-term solution that satisfied but for a moment.

This is how it works with something like porn as well. I admit that porn has not been a struggle for me, but I know from others who help men and women in their addiction to it that when you feed porn habits, the desire to view it and even act on what you're viewing grows. It is what happens with anything you feed—from an actual physical appetite for food in moments of emotion, to lust, perfectionism, alcohol, and so on.

This is also the way comfort satisfies us. It presents like the best friend we could ever have, promising the momentary soothing of a pain or problem. But in the process, it robs us of the real and lasting comfort we are looking for, often making it worse by delaying healing or piling on more issues to overcome.

Define *comfort* in your own words.

Look up *comfort* in an online dictionary, and write down that definition.

Recall a time in your life when comfort presented like a best friend but robbed you of something important by keeping you sedentary in your spiritual life, risk avoidant at work or in a relationship, or engaged in a negative lifestyle or habit that should have been addressed. Write down those circumstances.

How did that "comfortable" state keep you stagnant, denying you what you really wanted? What was your true desire?

If you think about the ways comfort has historically stolen from our lives, it makes sense that we would despise and resist it. In fact, I believe that *until* we see what comfort has taken from us, we will not hate it enough to let it go. But many of us exist in comfort-driven lives, year after year. Comfort is an idol that gets in the way of God reviving our souls; it prevents us from living the vibrant and fulfilled lives we long for—and it's often such a sneaky, subtle part of our lifestyle that we don't even see it. It's why it must be called out here.

Read the story of Jacob and Esau in Genesis 25:19–34.

Look at verses 29–30. What desire was Esau in tune with? How did he seek to comfort himself in that moment?

Look at verse 31. What exchange did Jacob propose?

Was it a worthy trade?

If not, why do you think Esau was willing to make the trade in the moment anyway?

What was the result, not only tangibly but emotionally, for Esau? (See v. 34.)

> The real issue... is seeking comfort in temporary fixes that often become gods (aka idolatry), which eventually come between us and the God of all true comfort.

Our quick response to be comforted by temporary efforts (food, porn, gossip, shopping, Netflix, alcohol, toxic relationships, fear, etc.) not only often harms us in visible ways, but it almost always results in emotional damage. It harms us spiritually as well. Here are the three ways comfort costs us big, even while pitching itself to us as the best friend we will ever have:

1. **Relationships with others:** When comfort becomes our god, we compromise the needed work required for good, healthy relationships with others. We will be less willing to mend fences, make the phone call, go first with an apology. We get comfortable with fractures and stubbornness. We settle for not serving one another, not forgiving one another, not loving one another as Christ so loved us. So it costs us relationship with others.
2. **Relationship with ourselves:** When comfort becomes our god, our self-worth suffers. Our hearts know we were meant for more, and we live in the tension between living safe and settled in and being unconventionally, joyfully free to serve Jesus. When we don't defy our comfort, it leads to a soul climate of apathy, which leads to guilt because we weren't meant to make so little of our lives. Our potential cries out within and it refuses to be silenced. This is why so many of us live with constant angst. It's why we often ask ourselves, "Why, with all the ways God has blessed me, am I still not happy?" Our souls weren't meant to be comforted by earthly things; they were meant to be comforted by God, even in the discomfort of a fallen world.

3. **Relationship with God:** When comfort becomes our god, we give up vibrancy in our relationship with the Lord. He doesn't leave us, but the fullness and abundance of all Christ has to offer us (see John 10:10 NIV, CSB) are compromised by our own unwillingness to go *all in*. Ask yourself these questions: *Have my comfort-driven decisions ever brought me closer to the Lord? Or have they ever kept me from doing things I sensed He wanted me to do?* This helps you see what comfort has cost you. If you are not living to your full potential, I would suggest it is likely not because you need another self-help book to help you know yourself better. Not if you're a believer in Jesus Christ. It is probably because your desire for comfort in some aspect has played a role in your unwillingness to obey the Lord in an area of your life. I would at least check there first.

Consider this chart. Describe how comfort has taken each of these important things from you in some way. You may have more than one example. It's important to name them. I'll go first with mine.

Relationship to Others	Relationship to Self	Relationship to the Lord
Broken relationship for 5 years with a friend	Shame for not conquering something	Not experiencing true vibrancy in relationship with God

Please don't misunderstand me. We need comfort in this world. (Oh boy, do we!) God loves us and wants us to be comforted. The real issue (and subsequently, the real problem) is not seeking comfort. It is seeking comfort in temporary fixes that often become gods (aka idolatry), which eventually come between us and the God of all true comfort. He is really who we are looking for, how our hearts long to be comforted, peaceful, fulfilled, and free. (We just reach for the crunchy tacos sometimes instead!) So I don't want us settling for a faux comfort that in the end not only doesn't truly comfort us but also, as in the case of Esau, ultimately breaks our hearts because of how it costs us even more *in the name of comfort.*

Let's close out with the truth, then. There are so many beautiful verses of comfort in the Word. Here are some I love—a variety about strength, hope, tenderness, care, and mercy. **Choose a few to read now, read them all in one sitting, or save some to read when you need them most!**

Exodus 14:14
Psalm 23:4
Psalm 32:7–8
Psalm 56:8
Psalm 116:2–4
Psalm 145:18–19
Isaiah 40:31
Isaiah 41:10
Isaiah 43:2
Matthew 11:28–30
John 14:27
Romans 8:28
Romans 8:38–39
Romans 15:13
1 Peter 5:7
1 Peter 5:10

DAY 3

What Do I Want?

As we look at this potential idol of comfort, I want you to remember it in the context of what we studied in the last session, from the interaction following John's preaching in John 1 and Jesus' subsequent question: "What do you want?" to His two immediate followers.

This is important because I can't help but wonder if the men would have been so quick to leave John's side and follow Jesus if He had flashed a quick picture of their comforts in front of them when asking the question. Comfort is a stubborn thing to abandon. We don't like losing the thing we feel is making life easier (even if it really isn't).

Revisit John 1:35–38 to refresh your memory of the passage.

What do you think some of the comforts a person in those times would have to "give up" to follow Jesus?

How would abandoning their comforts compare to abandoning ours today?

One thing that has always struck me about this passage is verse 37: "The two disciples heard him speak, and they followed Jesus" (NKJV). There is no pause in action here. They heard John's words; they followed Jesus. They didn't ask questions. They didn't say, "Please show some ID or prove Yourself in some way." They just followed. Was this the result of John's good leadership in getting them ready for Jesus' coming? Perhaps. Was it their own ready hearts? I would imagine so. Whatever the reason, they followed Jesus immediately. This shows both readiness and willingness. When we want God more than we want comfort, we do not hesitate to follow Him.

Complete the comfort chart by listing five things that you like the way you like them. What brings you comfort? Then beside each, list how this might change if you choose God over those comforts.

What gives me comfort?	How might this change if I choose God over comfort?

Did any of the answers in the "How might this change?" column feel negative or scary? (For example, "If I choose God over my comfort with alcohol, I'll have to go to rehab or come clean with my kids, and that terrifies me!") If so, do you believe that, ultimately, it is still the right choice? Why or why not?

What decisions or lifestyle changes will you have to make to choose God over comfort? Are you willing to make them?

I want to acknowledge your bravery to admit things that are hard. I also want to tell you that the first step to true freedom is being honest with yourself. If you are willing to do that, you will gain so much more than you ever fear losing. When I looked at the road in front of me—when I resolved to not shop for one whole year—it felt like a task I was destined to fail. I didn't want to tell anyone I was going to do it because what if I had a weak moment and "relapsed" during the year? But the Lord convicted me to share it publicly so I would have the accountability I needed to hold to my promise to Him not to shop for one whole year. I highly recommend being open with at least family and friends about your struggle and what you are doing about it, whatever your "comfort idol" is.

Who can you ask to help you or pray for you in these actions you need to take?

We can glean so much from the passage in John 1 in our desire for God over comfort. As I think about these disciples' pivot from following John to following Jesus, I think about our struggle to follow God at all. Instead of immediate obedience to follow God as these men did, we want immediate relief. We live in an instant-gratification society, where no-wait lines, no-hassle ordering, and no-strings-attached relationships have led us to demand that everyone from business owners to churches meet our needs right away. If they don't, we will leave and go somewhere that will, and other churches and businesses are just waiting for us. Because of this, we not only don't give God much of our time or attention, we give Him no time to work in our lives before running off the other way, looking for something quicker to give us the comfort and relief we crave and claiming He is not working fast enough.

How has your desire for immediate relief made it harder for you to connect to God and enjoy a more rooted relationship through the years?

> When we want God more than we want comfort, we do not hesitate to follow Him.

I love the way late theologian Eugene Peterson termed following Jesus in his book *A Long Obedience in the Same Direction: Discipleship in an Instant Society*—just the title tells you everything you need to know. Not only do we need to be quick to follow Jesus, but we must also be willing to go the distance with Him; I find that we are typically one or the other. We may be eager to jump toward Jesus—*Yes, Jesus, I will follow You!*—but slow to walk the journey out with Him—*Sorry, Jesus, I have to jump ship because I'm uncomfortable now as this gets harder!* Or we are slow to even commit because He seems to never be able to prove Himself worthy due to our continual skepticism and Band-Aiding that doesn't make room for Him to be Lord of our lives in the first place. Following Jesus is a call for both: the immediate obedience and the long obedience and in that, the abandoning of comfort as we trust God to be better and more.

Which has been more of an issue for you—the immediate obedience or the long obedience—and in what ways?

Speaking of Band-Aiding, please allow me a rather simple illustration.

When my middle son, Micah, was little and he got hurt, like so many little ones, he wanted to put a Band-Aid on everything. He didn't understand that a sprained ankle wouldn't heal with a Band-Aid. Neither would a bruise or even a cut. A Band-Aid might be a covering to prevent bacteria from coming in, but ultimately it wasn't going to heal anything.

The reason Micah wanted those bandages on things was mostly to not have to see his wounds.

Often, our comforts keep us from the temporary discomfort of seeing things we do not want to see, facing things we do not want to face. Our sins, for instance. Or even just hard things we don't want to tackle in the moment. In that way, comfort feels like it's doing us a huge favor by not making us confront discomfort. It temporarily bandages the problem, so we at least don't have to see it.

What are some areas of your life you either currently want to Band-Aid or have Band-Aided in the past so you didn't have to see them, instead of doing the hard work of seeking healing? Write them on this Band-Aid.

Saint Augustine is often credited with saying, "In my deepest wound I saw your glory, and it dazzled me." What if, instead of continuing to Band-Aid our issues, we would let God in and allow ourselves to see Him?

It really comes down to asking ourselves: Is the Band-Aid of comfort worth missing out on ...

- **knowing who we really are?** "These go-to comfort responses hurt us, because they keep us from finding out who we really are outside of them."[1] Deep down, we all want to know who we are and be who God made us to be. But comfort responses (aka Band-Aids) cushion us from our own reality, which keeps us from being fully self-aware and thus, fully honest with ourselves.

- **living in freedom and with a healthy perspective?** We are all searching for that magical moment of "arrival," when we have enough, know enough, *are* enough. But that's a lie. None of anything that ever comforts us will be enough, even the comfort of lying to ourselves. Comfort gives us the illusion of enough, but if we are honest—if we stop comforting ourselves long enough—we will see that it's not enough.
- **enjoying our full potential for Christ?** "Comfort is incompatible with serving. It is incompatible with radical living."[2] Comfort gets in the way of living out our full potential. When we experience a revival of the soul, finding ways to use our gifts and getting involved in things that make our hearts beat a little faster will not be a problem. The response to our want for God will be automatic. But comfort will not allow us to make even that first move.
- **knowing God intimately and gaining His godly insight?** This is where that "seeing the glory of God and it dazzling us" comes into play. "Comfort has cost us prayers in the night for those who are lost while we are lying in our beds scrolling on our phones. Comfort has cost us spiritual breakthroughs for our kids while we have spent hours on social media posting videos of them. Comfort has cost us seeing God work in amazing ways while we text our days away in complaints to friends about why our lives are a wreck.... Comfort keeps us from having godly insight, not because He does not want to share with us rich, beautiful things our human minds cannot know, but because of our lack of intention toward the knowing. God wants to let us in on so many things we would otherwise not know. But we don't pursue that. Our comfort won't let us."[3]

I'm taking my own inventory here. I feel the Lord's conviction in my own spirit. When you think of comfort in this way, it seems crazy to ever choose it over God. And yet, we often do.

Which of the above do you most yearn to restore in your relationship with God?

Write out a short prayer of intention toward God: "God, I want You more than the comfort of …" or "God, I want *to want* You more than the comfort of …" and pray it the rest of this week.

DAY 4

What Is in My Way?

We've already talked about some specific "comfort idols" that might be in your way. Or call them Band-Aids. You likely know what they are for you.

But sometimes there are some less overt things that come between us and God.

Let's start with a refresher on the word *comfort* itself, which you defined back on day 2. Here are some of my thoughts about comfort, based on my own experience:

- Comfort is the feeling of being safe, at ease, and relieved, free from mental and physical stress.
- Comfort can come from different sources—a warm bed or the warm embrace of a friend.
- Comfort is very personal. What's comforting to me won't necessarily be comforting to you.

I have to be honest and tell you that I love comfort! In fact, whether it is rushing home to get into my favorite pair of pj's, or slipping into my soft bed at night, or spending a few extra dollars on nice toilet paper at the store, I admit to being a comfort-driven person, as shown in my personal luxuries!

Don't hear that God is standing over us in judgment about how we spend our time or what we spend our money on. If you hear that, you are missing the point. It is that we, as humans, are bent toward distraction and self-indulgence by our very nature. So we have to fight our desire to simply live in a comfortable state if we are going to live with an *all-in heart* (which leads to an all-in life!) for God. Also hear this: The point is not a life of self-depricating martyrdom either (although our lives are meant to be lived for the kingdom and not for ourselves).

We are disillusioned, dissatisfied people in this world—*looking at us, Christian America*—beyond the discomfort we should feel in a temporary earth, because we have chosen ourselves and our own comfort. We are called to a life of sacrificial love as modeled by Christ, but it has seemed too hard, so we have chosen an alternate way. In the process, we have robbed ourselves of the full and thriving life! It seems counterintuitive, but it's been our preference.

In light of this conversation, how does the temporary, worldly comfort seem to you now—still like a best friend, or more like the sneaky foe? Journal your thoughts here.

How can you begin to see our God of comfort as the comfort you want instead?

So let's talk about the comforts that get in our way. We have been looking at them and naming the specifics, but I am going to circle back, zoom out, and talk about them in larger categories. It's important to do this because it may help us identify even more things we haven't noticed before—now or when they come up in the future.

1. The Comfort Idol of Indulgence

We want immediate comfort, so we look to indulge in whatever is closest to us, is offered to us, or feels the best to us, forgoing God's better way, which is often the less convenient or comfortable.

A lesser-known story in the book of Haggai is one I often revisit when thinking about this temptation.

Read Haggai 1:1–6. In your view, what is happening here?

A bit of backstory: The book of Haggai contains messages from God through the prophet Haggai, dating back to 520 BC, pertaining to rebuilding the Jerusalem temple and the people's future.

Though the book is short (just two chapters), it is divided into four such messages. The first message is a call to the Jews to finish rebuilding the temple. The second message predicts the future glory of the temple they are building. The third message reflects on how the people's impurity due to sin led to difficulties. The fourth message relates to God's choice of Zerubbabel as a leader of the community.[1]

In Haggai 1:1–6, the prophet Haggai was speaking to the people of Judah who were rebuilding the temple, but in the process, they became distracted by wanting to build their own homes. Because of that human desire, it had taken fifteen years longer, and the Lord noticed and sent Haggai to confront them. The vivid imagery in this passage powerfully illustrates the point.

Reread Haggai 1:4. Write down the question God asks the people. How does that speak to the comfort idol of indulgence?

Reread verse 6. What are the four specific "You … but …" examples Haggai gives?

You … But	Comforts Addressed

What visual image does Haggai use in the last part of verse 6? Draw it here.

How does picturing that help you see the false comfort of finding our security in work or earning money?

This passage in Haggai shows us that it's never enough—the houses, the food, the alcohol, the clothes, the work. In the end, or even in the interim, nothing we attempt to find our comfort in is enough. (Ever notice that it might seem like we have enough, but we still aren't happy?) What we know is that "enough" is only found in the all-in heart of wanting God and pursuing God most.

2. The Comfort Idol of Spiritual Apathy

At first, we might not think of spiritual apathy as comforting, but let me explain. We often settle for our comforting spiritual rituals and routines rather than an intimate relationship with the Lord. Talk about a Band-Aid. How many times, rather than getting alone and quiet with the Lord, allowing Him to do a more thorough but often harder private work in us, have we taken to inspiring others on social media with a posted Bible verse? Or put our heads down and gone right into church volunteer mode? These things can feel comforting, but they will not bring us true comfort.

"This was God's plan: to create humans with an innate longing for Him. It is why, then, try as we may, we can't ever be satisfied a different way. It's why a half-in, vanilla Christianity doesn't work or feel good. We can live this way for a time, but it will eventually eat away at our insides."[2]

You might imagine I would bring up the church at Laodicea in this moment. Undoubtedly, they are a good example of how not to become too comfortable and stale. Another one of the seven churches John's vision addressed in the book of Revelation, the church in Laodicea had grown lukewarm and unproductive. Their selfish focus on wealth and culture kept them from living on mission. But God desired relationship with them again, and that relationship would put the church back on mission.

Read Revelation 3:14–21. What was Laodicea's abundance preventing them from seeing?

What is your abundance not allowing you to see?

This is the main issue with comfort. It blinds us to the things we need to address, and spiritual apathy numbs us to letting God address them in us.

3. The Comfort Idol of Immediacy

This comfort idol troubled Esau in Genesis 25 (which we studied in day 2). We won't revisit it in detail again, but remember how in tune Esau was with his hunger pangs? Remember how he thought he was "starved," but the bowl of soup would only satisfy him temporarily until he needed to eat again? And yet, the comfort idol of immediacy enticed him to give up his entire birthright. In those days a birthright was the right of a firstborn to a larger (often double) inheritance than his siblings received—and other special privileges (Gen. 25:33; 1 Chron. 5:1; 2 Chron. 21:3).[3] So the trade was not worthy!

As we think about the principle of the greater desire we discussed in session 1, day 5, I would be remiss if I didn't mention its opposite. Often, we are people of the "now" decision: we want what we want, and we want it right now. We aren't willing to forgo what we want most—to delay for what we know is the better option—for what we want now. It's not just that we want to be comforted; we want to be comforted immediately. And we will do whatever we can to get that instant comfort and relief. The problem is, we sabotage ourselves and our future happiness and fulfillment for a temporary "bowl of soup."

Recall a time when you operated as a person of the "now" decision instead of operating in the principle of the greater desire. How did that affect you?

What have you learned from the difference or the outcomes?

4. The Comfort Idol of Self-Righteousness

This is, perhaps, the sneakiest of all comfort idols. What's interesting is that self-righteousness can make us feel comfortable in our position even during a discussion like this one—as if this were not our problem. We can be blinded to our own neediness of God. The truth is, we are all needy of God. The humblest soul—likely the soul that is walking closest to Christ—recognizes his or her unworthiness even while rejoicing in the constant transformative power of the Lord. There's a non-sense of self in it, not a low sense of self in it. As we properly elevate Christ, He fortifies our confidence in Him. This leads to a readjustment of our proper significance in the kingdom: not a self-loathing but a true insignificance. It is the most peaceful, confident way to live.

Read Romans 2:3–4 in *The Message* paraphrase.

What are your honest thoughts about these verses, particularly the statement "God is kind, but he's not soft"?

I absolutely love these verses in this paraphrase. As God kindly corrects us, His correction will often be firm. It won't be comforting, especially at first. But it will be thorough and for our good. We know this because Romans 8:28 promises us that His intention for us is for good. We also know that God cannot separate attributes of His character from each other, so as He corrects us, He also fully loves us and does so with our goodness in mind. Secular comfort cannot promise any of that. Not even a fraction of it. It will simply be the Band-Aid—covering something ugly so we don't see it—until it falls off or we swap it out for another Band-Aid. But always temporary.

There's nothing uglier than facing our own smug behavior. Self-righteousness is so very unattractive, and so it is to the Lord. He called it out many times in the Pharisees and Sadducees, religious leaders in their day (see Matt. 3:7; 16:1–4; 23:13, 23). Today we have plenty of people yelling to be more theologically astute and preaching Christ, but far fewer who want to dive into the everyday integrity issues that plague the church. It is both, my friend. Know your Bible. Know it to hide it in your heart and share it with others in your life—and perhaps on your stage—but not to throw around how smart you are. I'm praying for more and more people who are all knowledge and no heart to sit down and let God do a work so misguided spiritual leaders stop leading people astray.

> **Paraphrase:** "a rewording for the purpose of clarification ... in the same language as the source it is restating, and to reflect the same content, if not the same form, as that original source."
>
> **Translation:** "separate, and possibly divergent, translations from the same source ... equally valid expressions of what the translators understood about the author's intentions."[24]

I implore you: don't get comfortable in your self-righteousness. Even right now, though you might not see it or have yet to consider it, let the Lord call it out and dig it out of you so His kindness can lead you to repentance.

And on that note ... let's pray. We may have some work to do with the Lord before we start day 5!

Write out an honest prayer to the Lord, asking Him to reveal to you any sneaky comfort idol that might be in your way. Name each item on the list above, pause on each one, and ask the Lord if that is an area He needs to deal with you about. And then sit quietly, as long as possible ... and listen.

DAY 5

How Can I Have a Soul Revival?

Anyone who knows me knows how much I love my family. I am not shy to share about my children, even though they are now grown and do not let me gush on social media anymore. I've honored their wishes, but they've taken away a lot of great material in recent years. (I guess this means I just wait on grandkids?)

Through the years, though, I've had plenty of moments to test the theory for myself *to myself* about wanting God more than I want my desires. Where comfort is concerned, my comfort lies with my family. I want to be home around them—to enjoy hanging out, sharing meals, not missing out on their company. I have learned, though, that my feelings have to be processed in light of what I know to be true. If I am home with my family, I will feel the discomfort of not living out my calling to preach the gospel, which often involves travel. If that sounds like a tension, it is.

Though feelings should not make *decisions* for us, I am not a fan of *denying* our feelings. Pretending, denying, and even hiding our feelings has caused disastrous results for a lot of us—and the church is paying a high price for leaders (men in particular) who did not honor the feelings and wounds inside of us. At the same time, it's not a good idea to allow our feelings to drive our desires and our decisions either. We need a balance of working on and through feelings, naming them, and, in this case, determining how our desire for comfort is playing a role.

In the chart, write down a decision you're currently facing, a feeling you're having about it, and if God or comfort is your greater desire in this situation.

Current Decision	Feeling about It	God or Comfort?

Not only do I not like to leave home, but making me even less comfortable ... I do not like to travel. I especially do not like to fly. In fact, at one point, I was terrified. I would grip the sides of my plane seat for dear life, convinced the plane was going to crash and I would not make it back to the comfort of my home—to my people. There were times the fear was too great, and I thought, *I do not want to go out and speak anymore.*

Yet every time I would go and speak, God would profoundly minister to and through me. I could not deny what He was doing in my obedience. I did not stop feeling uncomfortable; I just kept going, despite it. And can I be honest with you? Years later, I am still not completely comfortable with flying. It feels like the skies are bumpier than ever. The pilots seem to be tenser. News shows just a fraction of the turmoil and complications of lost luggage, volatile travelers, and canceled flights.

But it's not just that. So many times, when I'm away serving the Lord in another state (or even another country), my family is having fun back at home. I will get texts with smiling pictures—them eating together around the table—or hear of them making plans for the next night, knowing I won't land until after the night is long over. I love hearing them talk about the fun (I've told them: please keep including me!), and I want them to all be together. But I miss out. The comfort pull in me wants to be home and be included.

Following Jesus is not a choice to be lonely. It is a choice to be single-hearted, which will sometimes be a faith exercised with God and you—alone. You are never alone with God. But you may do things without another human in this world, and in those moments, He will be enough. More than enough. Yes, even if you experience some form of loneliness.

How does thinking about loneliness in the context of experiencing it with the Lord rather than trying to eradicate it completely change something for you?

How does that comfort you?

I think the church does a disservice when we don't talk about living with emotions like this. We are certainly not robots. Paul lived with a thorn (2 Cor. 12). He never got rid of it. We preach too strongly about arrival. Arrival is heaven. Perfection is heaven. Until we get there, even while we pray for holiness and sanctification and rejoice when we have victory and make progress as God changes us on this earth, we live with discomfort. So perhaps we get used to some discomfort rather than try to spend our lives ridding ourselves of it completely.

As always, Jesus is our great example in this. He always chose the Father for comfort, even while living with emotion (He wept; He was angry; He sweat drops of blood; He was weary from fasting; He was tempted in the wilderness) and continued to serve faithfully and well.

What did Jesus choose in Luke 2:41–52? Why is this a significant choice that defines wanting to be all in with God more than comfort?

What did Jesus choose in Matthew 27:32–56? Why is this most incredible event the greatest significant choice that defines wanting to be all in with God more than comfort?

Practicing Soul Revival

The Lord has shown us the way. Now let's plug in our biblical soul revival formula from Revelation 2 to help us:

REMEMBER

Missionary Elisabeth Elliot said, "When obedience to God contradicts what I think will give me pleasure, let me ask myself if I love Him."[1] As you think about the pleasure that comfort might bring you, remember what the Lord has done in your life. Remember how He alone has comforted you in places nothing temporary ever could. Remember how much He loves you and how much you love Him, not for what He does for you, but for who He is.

REPENT

Good news. There's always a new moment to turn around and not choose comfort again, in this particular situation. You are safe to admit to God in this moment that you want the easier, more comforting path, but you ultimately want Him and the comfort He brings. He will be quick to help. (I highly recommend you pick up a copy of my book *The Hard Good* if you haven't already.[2] I believe it could help you!)

REPEAT

Comfort will lure you again and again in this life. Will you Band-Aid? Will you insulate? Will you choose comfort over God? Each time, you'll have to remember that God is your first love. Repetition forms habits—both positive and negative. When you form a habit of consuming things that are better for you, you eventually crave those things that are better for you. When you consistently do things that are good for you, you eventually feel good and don't want to go back to feeling bad. This is the beauty of how God intended things to work for us.

Reflect on your week. How might you remember, repent, and repeat this week in light of the conversation on comfort?

Remember	Repent	Repeat

Session 3

MORE THAN CONTROL

WHOEVER DWELLS IN THE SHELTER OF THE MOST HIGH WILL REST IN THE SHADOW OF THE ALMIGHTY.

Psalm 91:1 (NIV)

Memorize this verse this week by our repetition model.

To follow along in the *I Want God* book, read chapters 6–7.

DAY 1

Video and Outline

Stream the "More Than Control" (session 3) video (link on p. 17) and complete the session 3 outline below as you watch.

Group leaders: See the session 3 guide in the back (p. 193) for group discussion information.

- **With all the hardship of this world, the goodness of God doesn't always ____________________________________.**
- **We want God to make sense to us so that we can have some type of ____________________ over what is happening around us that we do not ____________________.**
- **It's the pull of control in us that presents in subtle ways through our frustration and even disillusionment that causes us to ask, ____________________________________?**
- **Coming back to God is sometimes ____________________ what you've been trying to ____________________.**

✦ When God seems to not make sense and things are out of our control, we can start to do one of these things:

1. We can ________________.
2. We can ______________________________________.
3. We can try to ______________________________________ ____________________.

✦ We think controlling is the way, but in the end, control:

- ________________________________.
- Leads to ________________________________.
- Creates ______________________________________.

✦ The principle of the greater desire: forgoing ___________________________ ________________ for _____________________________________.

✦ ___________ and __________________ are closely connected.

✦ When the Lord says, "Fear not," in places like Isaiah 41:10, He is not just calling us to ____ to Him; He is also calling us to ____.
Think about it like Him also saying, "Control not."

✦ We can know we are learning to __________________________ when we see ourselves trying to ____.

✦ ______________ is the action we need when we feel afraid.

✦ We know of God's great overcoming of this world, even as we live in a world that often doesn't appear to be in any control. God assured us of this for one purpose: so that ________________ we might have ______________.

DAY 2

What Is My Real Issue?

I remember reading a book called *Rare Bird* some years ago.[1] It was a story of a mother who lost her twelve-year-old son, Jack, to a freak drowning accident when he and his sister innocently went to a neighbor friend's house to play in the rain before dinner. The book was so genuine and raw, and its author, Anna Whiston-Donaldson, wrote tenderly about the fact that she had always prided herself on being the mom who controlled everything. She knew where her kids were and when. She knew what was happening at all times. She controlled her kids' lives and schedules and meals and calendars. That way, she thought, nothing bad would ever happen.

Except it did. When Anna's son drowned, she experienced enormous guilt for having allowed him to play in the rain. Of course, it wasn't a reckless decision. It wasn't a riskier thing to allow him to do, like bungee jumping or cliff diving or even something like playing contact football. When her son was alive, a young friend of his had died in a horseback-riding incident. Anna even shared her relief that nothing bad like that would happen to one of her kids since they weren't in horseback-riding lessons. So when a normal activity like playing in the rain resulted in tragedy, she was totally thrown for a loop. Even more than that, it brought the death of what was actually a smoke screen: the idea that she was controlling her world, when in fact, she was controlling nothing.

My kids were little when I read this book, and I remember the chill that went up my spine while reading about this mom's experience. She had outed perhaps my greatest fear by naming the false god of control. In some way, it was something that I, especially as a mother, always wished were true: that I could control my world or at least most of the elements in it.

I wanted to do that so the people I loved the most would be safe, happy, and healthy and so all of us would stay together.

It's not that those desires are wrong, it's just that they aren't ours to manage. Those things belong in the hands of God, and our attempts to control them will only result in pain and internal turmoil, if not interpersonal conflict with other people as we smother them with our "care."

Have you ever had a relationship you cared about so much you wanted to control it, but you wound up smothering it with your "care"? Write about that and what happened.

What might have happened if you had given that to God to manage rather than try to manage it yourself?

When our kids were little, my husband used to have this famous saying: "You can tell me what to do with them or how to do it, but not both." Apparently, I was being a little too bossy with my demands for him to diaper them and how to put that diaper on right. I didn't always love the saying at the time, but it did help give me a reality check to back off a little.

The truth is, I can also get bossy with God. Rather than ask or, better yet, just talk with God, I often tell Him what to do, how to do it, and even when to do it. I want my prayer answered by 6:00 p.m. the next day—earlier if possible. But my tendencies toward control severely get in the way of going all in with Him. I want to be in control, and that can be at odds with my desire for simply more of God.

Have you ever thought of your desire for control as being in direct conflict with desiring God? Think about it now and how that has affected your relationship with Him, and write down some thoughts.

We may not make this connection, but if we stop and think, we can see it: fear and control are inextricably connected. When the Lord says, "Fear not" (Isaiah 41:10 ESV and other places), it is not only a call to release our fears to Him; it is a call to surrender our control. In essence it is saying, "Control not." This is not a call to perfection, as we know that in our humanity both fear and control will be our work in progress until eternity. It is a singular message of death to flesh in exchange for trust in His sovereignty. It is linked together.

Instructions: List the things you want to control. Next, list your biggest fears. Then note where they overlap as a worst-case scenario.

Want to Control	Fears	Worst-Case Scenario	Reality
			God is in control
			God is in control
			God is in control
			God is in control
			God is in control

All this is an issue of our humanity fully relying on the God to whom we have given our lives—which we cannot control, as much as we wish we could. It is a hard surrender. But it is possible—and, I might add, necessary—to live a peace-filled life.

Because those who do surrender understand the exchange: control for assurance that we will ultimately be okay.

Look up the familiar verse John 16:33. What do the first two sentences of this verse say (in NLT)? Write them down.

Please note: This is a *when* statement, not an *if* statement. What does that mean to you?

What does the last sentence of this verse say? Write it down.

What does "overcome the world" mean to you?

There's a commonality of control in both parts of this verse. What is it?

Human control has no place in either of these aspects of life. We can neither control what happens to us nor overcome the world ourselves. At first, this may discourage us. But it shouldn't when we know and trust the Lord. As our memory verse says, in His shelter is the safest place to be.

Write down Psalm 91:1. Read it out loud two times. In what ways does this encourage you?

Like comfort, control can seem like a viable option in many of our life circumstances. In the moment, controlling things *feels* better. But in the case of control, it almost always causes a mess. When we're under stress or afraid, are we really thinking clearly? Do we have others' best interests in mind? The Lord has the better perspective—He is the one we should leave things to.

Read Jonah 1. How did Jonah try to control his situation in opposition to what God wanted? How did that result in a mess for himself (and others)?

Have you ever experienced a "Jonah" moment, thinking you had a better idea than God's?

Read Luke 10:38–42. **How did Martha's desire to control her environment and to be perfect get in her way of experiencing God?**

Have you ever experienced a "Martha" moment?

It is important to dig into what our real issues with control are, rather than make excuses for them. In a Martha moment, we might say, "I'm just organized" or "I just want my house to look good for company." Those things might be true. But perhaps it's more—maybe we aren't simply "just being our authentic selves." If we are loving the Lord but wanting our control more than we want Him, we will miss the beauty of experiencing moments with Him (and with others!).

In Jonah's situation, he missed ministry the first time around because he was afraid. Sure, he wound up going to preach, but it wasn't until after his ship had weathered a horrific storm, angry sailors had thrown him overboard, and he had spent days in a whale's stomach that he finally surrendered.

In Martha's situation, she missed something we would all probably die to experience. She missed the experience of hearing from the Lord Himself. And yet I wonder if many of us, in our quest to achieve a perfect aesthetic, wouldn't also miss God Himself if He walked into the room and sat down, ready to speak to us.

When you think of it that way, control doesn't sound like a very good idea, does it?

How would it grieve you to know you had missed out because you were too busy controlling things? Write down how it would make you feel.

Write a prayer of confession for your control, being specific, and asking the Lord to help you give over control to Him.

DAY 3

What Do I Want?

The biggest way our desire for control shows up in our spiritual lives is that we want God to be logical and reasonable. In short: we want God to make sense.

At a recent conference where I spoke, we invited people to send in questions during a Q and A time. About 85 percent of the questions were some form of "If God is good, why do bad things happen in this world?" (Since I've covered it in both *The Hard Good* and *Your God Knows* studies, I won't address it in depth here.) It's a fair question, since with all the hardship in this world, the goodness of God doesn't always make logical sense. We struggle to believe if God is even still with us at times, let alone that He's the good God He says He is.

Those feelings and thoughts are real. We are human, with limited knowledge and vision, so it is normal to wonder. But there is also a subtle undertone we don't like to address; we think in some way that if we were God, we would do things differently. (Oh, I know; you were surely not suggesting *that*!) It's the pull to control in us that presents in subtle ways through our frustration, questioning, and even disillusionment ... *Why isn't God doing what we want?*

So let's start by defining *control*. What is it, in your own words?

Now look it up in an online dictionary. Write down the definition.

Bring it closer to home. What does control look like in your daily life?

I have often wanted control of my career. If I take it deeper, I have wanted God to make sense of His calling on my life. In the early days of my writing, it seemed like I was writing for no reason. Few people were reading my books. Few people were asking me to speak. Was I wasting my time? Had I misheard God when I *thought* He had called me?

When God seems to not make sense and His reason is out of our control, we can do one of these things:

1. We can doubt.
2. We can become angry.
3. We can try to take matters into our own hands.

Add to this list. What else have you tried to do when God did not make sense and things felt out of your control?

What was the result?

Read Genesis 6. It did not seem logical that God would send a flood and that an ark would need to be built. What if Noah had tried to control the situation instead of trusting God? Write down your thoughts.

The book of Jeremiah recounts Jeremiah's struggle with God's call on his life to preach. There were not only plots against him, but also a massive lack of success in terms of the number of people responding to the message.

Jeremiah preached for forty years, and not a single person converted to the God of Israel. What if Jeremiah had tried to take control of the situation rather than staying true to what God had called him to do? Write down your thoughts.

Read Luke 5:4–11. It did not seem logical to cast nets on the other side of the boat when the fishermen had been fishing all night. What if the men had exercised their control and refused to participate, missing the blessing of abundance on the other side? Write down your thoughts.

Read John 6:1–14. It did not seem logical to feed five thousand people with a few fish and loaves. What if the boy had refused to give up his lunch, disbelieving God could do anything with this meager offering? Write down your thoughts.

If we really want to watch God work in our lives ... if we want our souls to be revived ... we are going to have to believe God and trust in Him for things out of our control. This means things that will often not make sense. This defies everything within us that wants to have things line up in our minds. It stretches us because it will mean trusting God for things out of our reach and abilities. We say we want God to do something radical inside us, but then we apply conditions. Do we truly want God to work miracles in our lives? If so, that will require us to take our hands off the wheel and give up control. Not kind of, but all the way.

We say we want God to do something radical inside us, but then we apply conditions.

One of the ways this shows up more covertly is with our need to find answers and control the flow of information we so prevalently have at our disposal. We can mistakenly feel that the more we know, the more we control our world and everyone in it. The more knowledge we have, the more we can protect those we love. Knowledge and information are good. But they aren't our saviors from life's heartaches and struggles. Our determination to control things through knowledge moves us away from necessary dependence on God.

How has the pull toward information and knowledge sometimes kept you from relying on the Lord?

The irony is, many times we think we are in control, but we are not. So many moms have told me they thought they were in control only to realize when their kids made a bad decision that they were not, in fact, controlling anything, as in the story I told you yesterday about the child who drowned. I've had friends tell me they thought they were in complete control of their careers until suddenly they lost the jobs they had worked so hard at that they never even took time off. Then they realized they were never in control, and in the end, being the hardest worker in the room didn't save them from losing their jobs.

My dear friend Jenn controlled everything about her body but wound up losing a four-year fight with colorectal cancer (ultimately winning by getting the prize of heaven!). She was the healthiest person I have ever known. She moved her body every day, never took in caffeine or unnecessary sugar, and ate almost entirely organic. But that didn't stop cancer from entering her body without permission. She couldn't control everything, though at one time, she probably thought she could.

Recall a time when you thought you were in control, but you (ultimately) were not. What did you try to make happen? What actually happened? What did you/can you learn from this situation?

Circling back to our topic yesterday, with the tie between fear and control, so often what we want is to control things so we can feel better about them. We want to know things so there will be no surprises and hopefully, no problems or pain. (We think if we can control the problems, then we can prevent the pain.) We think if we can understand God, we can predict what He will do, or maybe even manipulate life to make it turn out a certain way, or at least have insight into what is up ahead to brace ourselves for it. It sounds somewhat illogical to read it, and even more so for me to write it, but this *is* our train of thought. Let me break this mindset down a bit more.

- **I want to understand God logically.** If we truly want God, we must abandon our demand for logic. We have to want Him more than we want to understand Him, since intellect gets in the way of unvarnished love. When we demand that God make sense beyond what He chooses to reveal to us, we overstep our role and show our sense of entitlement.

What is your feeling behind wanting to understand God logically? Name it.

Now read Isaiah 55:8–9. Since God's ways and knowledge are not ours, what "right desire" can you replace wanting to understand God with, and what would that look like?

- **I want to feel prepared for whatever comes my way.** While it's good to ready ourselves in life, and Ephesians 6 even suggests how to armor up for battle, we know there are things we cannot predict or control.

Write out Proverbs 16:9. What does this verse mean to you?

- **I want to live on my own terms.** This is typically a life lived in the both/and, where we hold on to control of some things but we are willing to give up control of others. Peter followed Jesus but denied Him three times. He wanted to be a faithful follower, but he also feared the crowd.

Have you ever wanted to live life "both ways"? Write down what life was like when you tried to live like that, and why that won't work.

Sometimes our wants conflict. Often, our will has to die. But at some point, we have to want God more than we want to be in control. Do you?

DAY 4

What Is in My Way?

What is standing in your way of giving over complete control to God? That is the question you must settle.

We often shrug off—even laugh off—this issue of control. We joke about how women, especially, like to "control" things—from husbands to kids to friends to homes to every aspect of our environments. But is it really funny? How much has control cost us in our lives? I suspect it's led to some of the anxiety issues we face. The more we have wanted and tried to control things, the more anxious we have felt when the balls have dropped. And the more anxiety we've felt, the more we've turned to control as the solution to the problem. Yet it hasn't helped in either case—it's made matters worse.

That is for one simple reason: Only God can help our anxious hearts. The idol of control can only give us the temporary, false sense that everything is better.

In session 1, we talked about idols. How is control an idol for you?

We may know that control is what is in our way of the spiritual revival we seek, but what does that control specifically look like?

Describe two areas where you choose control over God. How do you attempt to stay in control over your life and even over God?

A favorite spiritual thought leader of mine, the late Henri Nouwen, is credited with this insight: "The journey to spiritual maturity is a journey from control to trust." We can know we are learning to trust God more when we see ourselves trying to control our circumstances less. We can gauge this especially during these historically control-seeking circumstances:

- **God's silence during hard times:** When we choose to trust God instead of trying to gain the upper hand of control over Him when He seems silent during difficulties, when He allows things we love to be taken away, or when He doesn't deliver on our expectations, we will grow and deepen our relationship with Christ.

Describe a time when you felt God was silent. You asked. Others asked. You saw no change. You heard no response.

How did that impact your faith (positively or negatively)? In these moments, what would it look like to want the presence of God more than you want answers?

- **Others' reactions to our decisions or obedience:** When we choose the path of God, the one less taken, other people react to their own unwillingness or conviction. It is difficult to disapprove of others and not try to control them. But when we take our hands off, something strong and important is happening within. We are learning to trust God with others' opinions.

Think of a time when you chose a path that others did not choose. Maybe it was something simple, like saying no to a night out with girlfriends because you promised to make your kids pizza. And perhaps your friends thought your "no" was a judgment on how they spend their time. Maybe it was something like saying no to a youth sports travel team in favor of attending church. And again, others reacted to their own unwillingness to make that same commitment. It might have been something big, like a yes to foster care or a big move of some kind—something others did not approve of.

How did others react (withdrawal, anger, jealousy, resentment), and how did it make you feel? Did it change your course of action moving forward?

- **Feeling misunderstood:** When we choose to trust God when people do not understand, it does wonders for the part of us that longs to control our image. So many issues of people-pleasing are tied to the fear of being misunderstood or misrepresented, and yet, it is impossible to control what people ultimately think of us. As kind as we are, there will always be someone who does not like us. As much as we explain something, there will always be someone who still heard something we did not say. Someone will always believe what they want to believe, even if it's untrue. This is the nature of people. We should believe the best about each other, but often we do not. Trying to control that in others is wasting precious time God has given us to use our lives for His glory.

Describe a time when you felt misunderstood. What were the feelings around that? What would have happened if you had trusted God with that misrepresentation?

Only God can help our anxious hearts. The idol of control can only give us the temporary, false sense that everything is better.

Oswald Chambers once wrote, "To be misunderstood is a common fate of all who have ever tried to do anything great or good."[1] And Jesus Himself knew this plight: "But despite all the miraculous signs Jesus had done, most of the people still did not believe in him" (John 12:37). Sometimes it's easier to see things in others than in ourselves.

Spend a few minutes writing about how these things have led to controlling moments in your life—perhaps recalling a specific recent moment. Then write out a prayer giving that over to God.

God's silence during hard times:

Others' reactions to your decisions or obedience:

Feeling misunderstood:

DAY 5

How Can I Have a Soul Revival?

When it comes to laying down the idol of control, if you accept the invitation for a soul revival—for a desire for God—you will find yourself also laying aside your exhaustion. I wonder: How does not being so exhausted sound to you?

I present this to you in these terms because I know well the reality and the ramifications of living with a controlling mindset. This mindset leads to a controlling mode of operation, and in both, a constant need to keep all the plates spinning. When a plate inevitably falls, there's a big problem. Someone is let down. You feel like a failure. You think you must spin the plates better next time. And the try-hard life tries harder again.

We don't need any more people trying any harder and running ourselves into the ground. What we need are revived souls, pursuing God, allowing Him to fill us with a supernatural indwelling of His Spirit, trusting Him with our lives. In this, we will watch our desire for control lessen as our trust for Him increases.

Before we close out this week's session, I want to address what I call "the bubble life" we try to build in an effort to have control. This exercise provides a visual of how we attempt to construct a controlled environment around people, situations, and things we want to control: so we don't lose them, so we can control what they think or how they feel, so we can get them to love us or love God. (Even though that's a wonderful thing, it's not our job to try to control their faith; it can even backfire. We are to help them come to know God through our witness and testimony!)

Write down all the people, situations, and things that you've tried to control inside this bubble. (For some of you, this bubble might not be big enough. No worries. Feel free to draw another one in your own journal.) Next to each thing you named, write a word that represents what you've tried to control about that person or thing.

This bubble, though possibly insulated for a time, will at some point become penetrated by life. There's not a bubble big enough or strong enough to withstand tough circumstances. Instead, life requires faith—trusting God even in the things we will never understand, the things we aren't supposed to understand but want to anyway. Faith that we will be okay without the bubble.

Practicing Soul Revival

Once again, let's plug in our biblical soul revival formula from Revelation 2 to help us as we think about it in the context of control:

REMEMBER

As you think about your walk with the Lord, recall His faithfulness to help you in ways you could not help yourself. Control has not been the lifesaver you were looking for. Even in the things you thought you understood, there have been more things you have not that have marked your life. You haven't been able to prevent hard times, no matter how good your human effort. Only God can provide for you the best plan for the best life.

> Revival comes with a surrendering of logic and, yes, control. It is holding open the hands and laying down the need for reason. It is a deference to the heart and mind of God and the willingness to receive from Him even that which does not make sense. It is grasping on to the illogical sureties that God will provide even in the desert. That He will be enough in moments that nothing else is. We will never see God in the way we want if we hold on to a solo reliance upon our logic. Revelation doesn't come to closed hearts and minds.[1]

REPENT

How have you trusted in your control and not in God's sovereignty? Now is the time for the about-face. Remember that repentance is the great coming back together—the beautiful connection back to God. Repent of trusting in something that could and would—can and will—fail you: your abilities, ideas, clever strategizing, and the thought that you yourself hold anything together in your life. Repent of living in the bubble and thinking that anyone or anything you put inside it will be safe from the realities of living in a fallen and out-of-control world.

REPEAT

Controlling behavior dies hard. So many of us have been developing these ways for a very long time. We will have to keep working at trusting God, keep building up our spiritual muscles, keep preparing our hearts and lives with the steadfast belief that He doesn't have to make sense to be sovereign. You'll need to revisit the bubble often. On a monthly basis, look back at your bubble and ask, *Am I walking by faith or living in this bubble? Who or what else am I trying to keep "safe" inside the bubble? What would it look and feel like to pop the bubble and live free in the safety of trust in God?*

Reflect on your week. How might you remember, repent, and repeat this week?

Remember	Repent	Repeat

Session 4

MORE THAN POPULARITY

I AM NOT TRYING TO PLEASE PEOPLE.
I WANT TO PLEASE GOD.

Galatians 1:10a (CEV)

Memorize this verse this week by our repetition model.

To follow along in the *I Want God* book, read chapters 8–9.

DAY 1

Video and Outline

Stream the "More Than Popularity" (session 4) video (link on p. 17) and complete the session 4 outline below as you watch.

Group leaders: See the session 4 guide in the back (p. 195) for group discussion information.

- **The idol of ____________________ is really about ____________________ ______________________________________.**

- **There is a cycle of popularity that happens:**

    - **We want to be ____________ ▶ which creates ____________ ▶ which dictates our ____________ ▶ so we live as __________________________.**

- **Here's how popularity (aka, the approval of man, people-pleasing) affects us:**

    1. It changes ______________________________________ ________________________.

2. It changes the ______________________ we are willing to hold and the ______________________ we are willing to have.
3. It changes our ______________________ and can form ______________________.

✦ John 12:43 sums it all up well when he writes of the Pharisees: "They loved ______________________ more than ______________________ ______________."

✦ We crave these things:

1. ______________________: to feel part of something important, part of a group, part of a family
2. ______________________: to be loved for who we are, fully, completely, without strings, parameters, or conditions
3. ______________________: to be recognized in our uniqueness, thoroughly understood
4. ______________________: to leave a legacy and feel as though we matter

✦ It's not wrong to want to be ______________, ______________, ______________, or ______________________, but when we want it so much we are willing to seek those things by means other than God, we take matters into our own hands and it often goes wrong.

✦ The one who is ______________ of your soul's desire is the one who ______________ you and ______________ you most.

DAY 2

What Is My Real Issue?

My daughter and I have a core memory of attending a concert together when she was a tween. The musical artist, who will remain unnamed but has the initials J and B, was my daughter's absolute favorite. At the time JB had not hit his rebellious stage and was still sporting virgin skin with no tattoos, still singing relatively harmless songs about teen love and the angst that goes with it.

But make no mistake about it: his star had risen to the heights that no young man his age should have known. The concert was full of pyrotechnics, elaborate stage props, and most of all, screaming fans. JB could barely sing above them. In the opening act, he dropped down from the ceiling in massive wings as confetti shot into the audience from undetectable cannons all over the arena. To say it was an experience is an understatement.

About halfway through the concert, the massive screens behind JB began to play, showing him when he was little, in a homemade movie, playing makeshift "drums" on his kitchen chairs. It was a darling sight to watch this now much older version who had turned into a global superstar be transformed back into his humble start. I couldn't help but notice how very talented he was, even at that young age. He had an incredible voice and rhythmic timing from the time he was little.

Now that little boy had turned into an empire. His music had become a media machine.

As I sat there watching the video and taking in the concert, the juxtaposition between what was then and what was now had me thinking: *I wonder if JB ever wishes it was just about the music again. I wonder if he longs for that simpler time—if he could rewind time to live in that space where it hadn't become something else altogether.* Sure, he had so much more now. He had it *all*, in the eyes of most people. But did he really? Because once fame had set in and people were managing his career, it had to have changed everything. Now it was about the people he was servicing—he couldn't just do what he wanted anymore, even musically. His popularity required him to continue to please the people who bought his music, bought tickets to his concerts, and came to see him play the songs *they* loved and sang along with. In the moment, it seemed like it was all about him, but really, most of it wasn't about him anymore. It was all about them ... us ... the crowd he needed to please.

As I write this, you might be thinking, *What does a famous musician have to do with me in my regular life?* At first, you might not see the connection. But popularity has the same ramifications for all of us; it changes important things—especially how we go all in with God. (Hang on; I'm going to talk all about this in a minute.)

First, I want you to define *popularity* in your own words.

Now, how does an online dictionary define it?

I think it's important to not let the word *popularity* itself become a hindrance in this discussion. A lot of us were not popular in high school, so we immediately excuse ourselves from this conversation, thinking, *I wasn't popular, so Lisa isn't talking to me.*

Or we think, *I'm just a regular mom. I don't even have social media. Who is there to be "popular" with? This word doesn't even relate to my life.*

I understand these sentiments. I was not the most popular girl in school, so that situation certainly does not resonate with me ... and before I started writing, I had no kind of public following. I lived a life of diapering babies, fixing dinner, and eventually driving carpool and attending my kids' ball games as a bleacher mom. So I understand not relating to the idea of popularity.

But consider this definition of popularity: the quality of being approved of, favored, accepted, or admired. Popularity can be based on a variety of factors, such as physical appearance, social status, intelligence, talent, or charisma. Now are we hitting closer to home?

Thinking of this definition of *popularity*, how has your desire to be approved of, favored, accepted, or admired played out in your life and relationships?

How much did you struggle with wanting to be "popular" in these terms in the past? How much do you struggle with it in the present?

I do not consider myself to be a huge people-pleaser, but at times I still crave others' approval. In fact, I've been noticing it in myself much more. In the way I might beat around the bush instead of just telling someone no to an invitation. Overcommitting myself. Being partially but not completely honest when someone asks me for feedback, because I don't want to "hurt their feelings." Staying in a situation longer than I want, even if I know it's no longer healthy for either side, because it's just easier than cutting that tie. We can call it all kinds of things, but at the end of the day, it is that we don't want to lose favor—aka, popularity—with someone or a group of people.

So don't hear this word and assume it's about you running for prom queen. Or you trying to get a bunch of followers on Instagram. Or you wanting to become famous. No. It's you ... me ... us ... regular people ... wanting to be liked and approved of, and yes, possibly admired, to the point that it has taken seed in our hearts and minds and come out in our behavior. We want to be popular. That desire, then, serves a certain agenda. It dictates what we feel we must do. It takes away our ability to live without an angle. It tells us we must live to serve people so they stay happy *with us*. That removes the purity of how we live our lives and conflicts with living our lives for the kingdom of God. Doesn't sound very harmless, does it?

Consider this endless popularity-progression cycle:

How has this been true in your life? Write down some of the relationships this has affected.

Whom have you sought approval from to the point that it has changed how you acted?

Our desire for popularity changes the core of who we are. It becomes about living to please other people rather than living to please the Lord. Let's unpack what results from focusing on what our followers or neighbors want us to do rather than on how God wants us to live our lives.

It changes what we want and fight for.

In our Bible verse for this session (Gal. 1:10), Paul was writing to the church at Galatia, talking about how off mission he would be if his goal was anything but serving Christ in preaching a strong message that was contrary to the message others were preaching. The easier, more popular thing to do would have been to preach what people wanted to hear. But that has never helped anyone.

I wanted my one fight to be for getting people to love God, not to pursue having them love me.

The Lord spoke to my own heart about this years ago when I was in a season of wishing to be more liked. He showed me how that desire was causing me to drift into unhealthy habits, like overapologizing for my gifts, overexplaining myself when no explanation was needed, and neglecting to set good boundaries. He reminded me that He has created humans with a limited capacity for things like time and breath, and as a result, we will only have enough of both for one fight in life. We will either spend our lives fighting for people to love us by constant striving in people-pleasing, or we will fight for people to love the Lord by spending our lives sharing the good news about Him. I knew then that I wanted my one fight to be for getting people to love God, not to pursue having them love me.

How has wanting to be liked or approved of ever changed what you "fight for" (or caused you to back off from a worthy fight)? Write down a situation you can recall and what that looked like.

It changes the convictions we are willing to hold and the conversations we are willing to have.

When our desire to be liked and admired takes over, we will shy away from the important and often hard conversations we need to have, for fear that people will no longer love us if we hold to a different conviction. The fact is, they may need to hear that differing perspective when delivered in truth and love.

Describe a time you were tempted to water down a conviction or shy away from a conversation because you wanted to be accepted or admired.

It changes our dependence on God and can form pride within us.

When our eyes are on the prize of becoming popular, and if we succeed, it lessens our focus on the true goal of growing in the wisdom and humility of becoming like Christ. We receive our confidence from how others perceive and endorse us rather than from God's approval of us.

Have you ever gotten caught up in feeling confident about how others have endorsed you to the point that you became prideful about it? Did anyone notice and call you out?

No matter how it has shown up in your life, craving popularity truly is a futile chase. I remember reading this statement somewhere: "Popularity is a fickle thing. It comes and goes like the wind. It is based on outward appearances and superficial qualities. True worth comes from within, from our character, and our relationship with God."

Amen and amen.

The chart below represents your relationship with popularity. I'll use mine as an example of how to start. On days 3 and 4, you'll come back to this chart to add your "befores" to the columns. Then on day 5, I'll ask you to add your "afters." Check back to see if you've been consistent in the changes—with the Lord's help!

Popularity Statements

Before	After
I hope you like me.	Like me or not, I pray you cannot deny the presence of God in my life.
I hope I don't get canceled.	I cannot be silenced due to someone's disapproval when I never spoke out to gain anyone's applause.

DAY 3

What Do I Want?

When was the first time you remember wanting someone's approval?

My earliest memory of this was in the sixth grade, when I so badly wanted to win the friendship of a girl in my class named Emily. I was the new girl in town, desperately wanting to fit in, and Emily was cool. She was also kind of mean. I remember not wanting to get on her bad side.

I also vividly remember owning a beautiful lavender dress with silver thread running through it and a ruffled high-neck collar. (It's funny what your brain never lets you forget.) Even at that young age, I loved to be a bit on the fashion edge, and this dress certainly was that. Emily loved the dress as much as I did. I wore it to a special art night at our school, where we all dressed up and showed our parents the art we had made. One day shortly after, as we played on the playground, Emily came right up to me and said, "Hey, Lisa. I want that purple dress you wore at the art night. Bring it tomorrow to school and give it to me!" And with that, she turned around and left.

I thought about it for a few days, and Emily continued to ask me about it. I loved my lavender dress so much. But I wanted to be Emily's friend more. So I decided to give it to her. The next day, through a few tears, I folded up my dress, put it in a bag, took it to school, and sorrowfully handed it over to Emily.

When was the first time you remember wanting someone's approval? Write down who it was, what was happening, and how the events made you feel (in the process and in the end).

What's interesting about the popularity/approval process is that it doesn't feel as good as we hope. I thought once I gave the coveted dress over to Emily in exchange for her affection, it would feel worth it. But it didn't. I just felt sad that I had handed the dress over. And even if she *was* happier with me for the rest of that school day, it was short-lived. The next day I watched her skip off to lunch with her new best friend, who had complimented her on her haircut, which I was sure would go nicely with that purple dress I had given her to complete the look.

Recall a time when getting someone's approval resulted in disappointment. Write down the details of that situation.

It is crucial to ask yourself what you are really looking for in life, and if you believe jumping through hoops to become accepted by those who can change their minds on a dime about you—people with hormones, attitudes, conflicting feelings, biases, and issues of their own—is a good idea. In my view, not unless you like living in frustration.

I wrote this in the *Jesus over Everything* Bible study: "If your goal in life is to be liked and accepted by everyone, welcome to a life of exhaustion."[1]

You might need to read that sentence again.

Describe the exhaustion you feel when you are chasing the goal of people's approval. Why do you think this results in exhaustion?

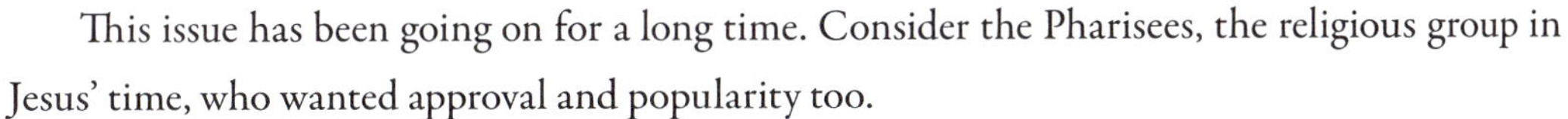

This issue has been going on for a long time. Consider the Pharisees, the religious group in Jesus' time, who wanted approval and popularity too.

Write out Matthew 6:2. What was the issue (tied to their approval seeking) Jesus was calling the Pharisees on the carpet for?

Write out Matthew 23:5. What were the Pharisees doing to get noticed?

Write out Luke 18:11–12. What was the Pharisee in this passage doing for his own popularity, and in what way did that offend God? (See also v. 14.)

Write out John 12:43. What did the Pharisees love more than the praise of God?

The truth is, what we really want deep down is often only temporarily satisfied in these moments of approval. Core needs like these:

- **Acceptance**—to feel a part of something important, part of a group, part of a family (this is why church and community are so important)
- **Unconditional love**—to be loved for who we are, fully, completely, without strings, parameters, or conditions
- **Being known**—to be recognized, fully and completely
- **Significance**—to leave a legacy and feel as though we matter

Which of these core needs resonates the most with you? In what ways?

It's not that wanting these things, as basic needs, is wrong. All of us long to be accepted. We want unconditional love, and we want to be known and seen. We want to feel as though our lives have meaning. We will just never find satisfaction for these needs in constantly chasing after popularity. These are issues of much greater depth than offering a favorite dress to someone can solve.

Because the truth is, those who need us to give them something in exchange for their acceptance and love will always put us in the position to chase their approval. And no one but God can really, truly know who we are in the private places of our minds, hearts, and souls. Consider these verses from the New International Version:

- "Before I formed you in the womb I knew you, before you were born I set you apart." (Jer. 1:5a)
- "For you created my inmost being; you knit me together in my mother's womb." (Ps. 139:13)
- "You have searched me, LORD, and you know me." (Ps. 139:1)

- "You discern my going out and my lying down; you are familiar with all my ways." (Ps. 139:3)
- "Before a word is on my tongue you, LORD, know it completely." (Ps. 139:4)

And though people *can* make us feel significant at times, no one can ever truly give us the feeling of significance we need for the long run.

Only God.

Now that you better understand the nature of your need for popularity, return to the chart on page 128 and add some more of your own "before" statements to it.

DAY 4

What Is in My Way?

How are you with popularity and approval comfort idols?

By now you know the drill: we look at the things we want more than God through the lens of idolatry, because that's what it is. By calling it what it is, we can help our souls experience lasting freedom from it.

For many of us, our decision making has been the clearest indicator of how much our desire for popularity has interfered with our lives. When face to face with our choices, we cannot deny they have been made with the hope of gathering people's affections in mind, whether or not that plan was successful.

Describe a time you allowed your desire for approval to dictate a decision. What does this reveal about your need for approval?

How different would your life look if you truly valued God's approval above everyone else's? What choices might be different?

> We look at the things we want more than God through the lens of idolatry, because that's what it is. By calling it what it is, we can help our souls experience lasting freedom from it.

In addition to our decision making, here are some other ways the desire for popularity shows up in your day-to-day life:

1. Weak or nonexistent boundaries and saying yes to things when you wanted to say no.

   What are ways you've struggled to set boundaries because your yes involved a desire to please people?

2. Worrying too much about what others think of you.

   Can you remember a time when you chose not to speak up because you chose human praise and acceptance over Jesus? Describe how you felt after the choice was made.

   Name two practical ways we can silence the voices of others and instead focus on God.

3. Overexplaining or overapologizing behavior.

When was the last time you overexplained yourself to another person? How did he or she receive it? How did you feel at the time you were doing it and after? Why might the behavior prove futile?

All these things ...

- serve as a distraction
- change the core of what we want and fight for
- change what we are willing to face and the conversations we are willing to have
- dictate what we feel we must do
- have exhausted us by trying to "keep" others happy
- cause us to potentially miss the voice of God

Now that you better understand the nature of your need for popularity, return to the chart on page 128 and add some more of your own "before" statements to it.

DAY 5

How Can I Have a Soul Revival?

Revival in the area of popularity will enable us to "be content with obscurity, like Christ" (Col. 3:4 MSG). This does not just apply to being known or famous. It means we are no longer enslaved to people. I don't know about you, but in this world full of surplus opinions (and often negative ones), I love the idea that I am not tethered to the opinion of anyone else. As always, thank You, Lord, for modeling the better way by living the example of contentment in the quiet life of being known only by You (and it being enough).

Read Colossians 3:4 from *The Message*:

> Your old life is dead. Your new life, which is your *real* life—even though invisible to spectators—is with Christ in God. *He* is your life. When Christ (your real life, remember) shows up again on this earth, you'll show up, too—the real you, the glorious you. Meanwhile, be content with obscurity, like Christ.

Write down your thoughts about this passage.

What does *real* life look like? How would you live if Christ were your life? What is one step you can take toward being content with obscurity?

The real character of life is not how much we can serve God in the spotlight. That is not hard, though it may stretch us to use our gifts in ways that feel beyond our capabilities (especially at first). When you are getting applause for what you do for the kingdom of God, it mostly feels exhilarating, since humans are bent toward seeking attention for themselves. But what about when you are doing the hidden, unseen work?

Many times, those are the moments when we grow closer to Christ. When our soul is revived.

In my own life, when God has placed me in seasons where I was serving without recognition, I grew spiritually in a different way. I experienced the Lord in a private, quiet place of reverence. I learned more about His heart—my own heart expanded for the people He loves. It's not that you cannot experience God in the spotlight, but I've lived in both spaces, and I can attest that you do not experience Him the same. Without the added "benefit" of man's approval, we are free to enjoy the pleasure of the Lord in our pure and simple service to Him.

Practicing Soul Revival

So let's focus once again on our revival formula from Revelation, with an emphasis on popularity:

REMEMBER

When we seek approval and popularity rather than God, we leave our first love, replacing Him with self. We are all created usable by God, but not everyone gets used. Our desire to be popular with other people hinders God's movement in us. God will let us choose ourselves over Him, and if we do this, He lets us have our way. As you think about your life with the Lord, remember His faithfulness to love you and accept you just as you are. Only God can give you what you need every day and in the depths of your soul.

Describe a recent decision that you can now see had more to do with seeking popularity than with following God.

REPENT

As you think about where you have chased other people's approval rather than sought after the Lord, take it to Him in earnest prayer and ask for His forgiveness. He is ready and willing to love you and take you back.

Choose one area where your actions reflect a desire for popularity—people-pleasing, image management (just to name a couple). How might you about-face in that area? What would it look like to change?

REPEAT

"God-courage doesn't just come. It doesn't just casually slide into our lives while we are busy chasing other things. It comes by one choice today to be brave. And then another brave choice tomorrow. And then, the next time the hard choice comes around, we find we have the courage to make it. But we have to choose that first time."[1]

What is one choice or change you need to make today? How can you move toward "God-courage" to ultimately help you with your need for approval?

Now that you better understand the nature of your need for popularity, return to the chart on page 128 and add your potential "after" statements to it.

Reflect on your week. How might you remember, repent, and repeat this week?

Remember	Repent	Repeat

Session 5

MORE THAN BLESSING

BLESSED BE THE GOD AND FATHER
OF OUR LORD JESUS CHRIST,
WHO HAS BLESSED US IN CHRIST
WITH EVERY SPIRITUAL BLESSING
IN THE HEAVENLY PLACES.

Ephesians 1:3 (ESV)

Memorize this verse this week by our repetition model.

To follow along in the *I Want God* book, read chapters 10–11.

DAY 1

Video and Outline

Stream the "More Than Blessing" (session 5) video (link on p. 17) and complete the session 5 outline below as you watch.

Group leaders: See the session 5 guide in the back (p. 196) for group discussion information.

- **The way we see ____________ is tied to the way we ____________ ____________________ in our lives.**
- **A right view of blessing:**

  1. **It comes from ____________________.**
  2. **It's rooted in ____________________.**
  3. **Blessing is ultimately ____________________ ____________.**
  4. **Blessing is directly tied to the benefits of ________________.**

- **Sometimes the reason we don't feel blessed is because ____________________ ________________.**

✦ Not feeling blessed is often due to our ____________________ rather than our ____________. This can be because of one or more of these things:

1. ______________________________________
2. ____________________________
3. ___________________

✦ When it comes to blessing, we have a ______________________________ of what it is and how God wants to bless us in ____.

✦ As a result of skewed understanding, we form a _______________________ relationship with God, which has two negative effects:

1. It becomes or stays very ____________________. (As we center on how we can get more, we become more and more inward focused. The result = pride.)
2. It robs us of ____________________ with the Lord, and in the end, we miss _________ blessings. (When we misunderstand true blessings, we may miss the package[s] they come in that we are not expecting. The result = disappointment and a lack of true joy.)

✦ We've all had times when we've settled for a transactional relationship with the Lord, but God is ready and waiting for us to ____ and come back to ____.

DAY 2

What Is My Real Issue?

My friends Mark and Susie are precious to me, though I have only seen them a handful of times since I was a teenager. They are a part of my childhood, as Mark was my beloved first youth pastor, and when he married the most beautiful redhead in the world, in my mind they became like a royal couple. But it was more than just being in awe of them. They inspired me by how they wanted God more than anything, and their life was built on Him.

Turns out social media is good for something, connecting me for years to this Texas couple who have spent their lives serving their city, other American cities, and other parts of the world. Once, when I was traveling through San Antonio, I reached out to them and they invited me over for dinner and to stay for the night. We spent hours catching up, talking about their many adventures serving the Lord. I can barely believe some of the stories they told me, they are so spiritually radical.

One thing I know about Mark and Susie: they do not live an extravagant life. Their home is wonderful but modest. Many of their stories include God's provision when they did not have enough to make ends meet but continued to pour out in service to others. Mark is a communicator, with many friends all over the world, but he is not famous. He and Susie have gathered a large community by serving people, not by having their names shared all over social media.

Are Mark and Susie blessed? That depends on your definition. They don't enjoy the world's exorbitance, so the world might say no. No elaborate house, fancy car, or great wealth. But they have a beautiful, long-running marriage. They serve the Lord together and have for years. They feed people. They have joy. They have watched the Lord do incredible things in and through them in their lifetime—miracles in front of their eyes. Now you tell me: *Are they blessed?*

How do you define the word *blessing*?

How is it defined in an online dictionary?

Describe someone you view as "blessed." What does their life look like? What kind of personality do they have, what do they talk about, what is their relationship with the Lord like?

Has your definition of *blessed* changed over the years? If so, how?

It's not that material things are not blessings. They certainly can be. It's just that defining blessings in physical terms does not capture all that they are, and I would daresay, not predominantly what they are. Since physical, material things can be fleeting and often dependent upon circumstances at least partially out of our control, they are not perfect indicators that God is blessing us. I've seen churches that I believe to be very blessed that were few in number. Were we to judge by secular measurement, we would say God is not bestowing favor there. But I would firmly disagree.

And martyrdom for the kingdom could certainly be an extreme but solid example. Many who have been martyred for the gospel of Jesus had a very different outcome than that of a "prosperity preacher" today. If we look at earthly standards, the more blessed is the one with the private jet and the lavish lifestyle. And yet, who is really more blessed? (We will get to this in a minute!)

> Everything we seek and do and ask for as believers in Jesus should be with the ultimate purpose of furthering the gospel, not our own little kingdoms.

So let me break it down. We often think we need to be heady, but sometimes, because Satan can be very confusing, it's good to get down to the basics of what we are really talking about here. So for clarity's sake, blessings can be:

- **material**, such as food, clothing, and shelter (and possibly "extras" as well)
- **spiritual**, such as forgiveness of sins, spiritual gifts, wisdom, and so on
- **emotional**, such as peace, joy, fulfillment, hope, happiness
- **relational**, such as family, friends, a spouse
- **vocational**, such as a job that is meaningful and fulfilling

What would you add to this list? What blessings have you personally enjoyed that are listed here? Pause and thank the Lord for them!

But let's make a slight (or not so slight), important shift.

Thinking about blessing in terms of wanting to be blessed by God more than wanting God Himself makes for an interesting conversation. It might not be one you've considered before. You may have even put them together rather than pulled them apart. After all, isn't it good to want God to bless us? Consider Jabez, who prayed a famous prayer in the Bible for God to bless him and expand his territory. (And God did!) "Jabez called out to the God of Israel, 'If only you would bless me, extend my border, let your hand be with me, and keep me from harm, so that I will not experience pain.' And God granted his request" (1 Chron. 4:10 CSB).

This request was not out of the blue. Jabez was a person of character and prayer, so his request was not for self-seeking glory but was one that aligned with God's heart for kingdom expansion. This is something we often miss in looking to the prayer of Jabez and the idea of blessing itself. Everything we seek and do and ask for as believers in Jesus should be with the ultimate purpose of furthering the gospel, not our own little kingdoms. With that context, asking to be blessed looks a bit different.

Considering blessing, and particularly the prayer of Jabez in this proper light, how does asking God to bless you look a bit different?

The real issue is that God wants us to want Him for Him and not for what He can do for us. He wants us to be hungry to serve the kingdom of God and rejoice in living in the benefits of the fullness that He so lavishly pours on us in His goodness as a good Father. We don't live to get blessed and tack on serving God and loving God at the end. Unfortunately, though, many of us do. But that's backward.

When we prioritize our want of blessing over our want of God, our relationship with God can turn into a transaction: *I will do this so You will give me that.* God becomes a genie or a vending machine to us: *Meet my request, please.* The result is a shallow relationship with the Lord. A transactional relationship with God has two negative effects:

- **It becomes or stays very self-focused.** As we center on how we can get more, we become more and more inward focused. The result equals pride.
- **It misses true blessings.** When we misunderstand true blessings (fruit of the Spirit, benefits from God as outlined in Psalm 103, etc.), we miss God's true gifts to us, which may not come in the package(s) we are expecting. The result equals disappointment and a lack of true joy.

Which of these two resonates most with you and why? How has your focus on the "blessing" had you missing God?

As we dive into the "real issue" (our focus), here are four truths about a right view of blessing:

- A right view of blessing comes from spiritual maturity—only then will we have a right lens.

Write down 1 Corinthians 13:11. Though in the context of love, how does this apply to what happens when we spiritually mature in our view of blessing?

- A right view of blessing is rooted in the Bible—not in culture.

Read Matthew 6:1–6. How do these verses apply to the right view of blessing?

- Blessing is ultimately for heaven, not for earth.

Write down Matthew 6:19–20. Why is blessing in the future ultimately for the best?

- Blessing is directly tied to the benefits of God Himself.

Write down Psalm 103:2.

With your Bible (or Bible app) open to the entire chapter of Psalm 103, write down all the "benefits" you read of God Himself.

As we have done every week, on day 5 we will "remember" as part of our soul revival practice. Looking at a passage like Psalm 103 and writing down all the benefits of God is a powerful way to practice the spiritual discipline of remembering God. When we do, it increases our desire for Him. We cannot help but remember His many benefits to our lives and want Him for Him, not to get His blessings but to get God, the blessing *Himself.*

I hope by now you've heard what the real issue is: the irony of wanting God for God is receiving the blessing you have truly been looking for.

DAY 3

What Do I Want?

You might remember in 2020 when the song "The Blessing," (by Kari Jobe, Cody Carnes, Chris Brown, and Steven Furtick) made its debut in the world and so many Christians fell in love with it. I can remember the first time I heard it, hitting replay multiple times, turning the volume up, and worshipping in my kitchen.

Yes to God blessing me. Even more yes to the idea of God blessing the generations in my family. Yes to God giving us peace. Especially during a year of turmoil, pain, and destruction, these things were literally music to our ears.

"The act of blessing is rooted in Israelite culture and comes in several forms. A divine blessing, as found in Numbers, was a part of everyday language for greeting one another and placing God's name on His people."[2]

But this song wasn't the concept of these talented songwriters. It was straight from the Bible, from Numbers 6:24–26: "The LORD bless you and keep you; the LORD make his face shine on you and be gracious to you; the LORD turn his face toward you and give you peace" (NIV).

This "priestly" blessing, or "Aaronic" blessing, as it's also referred to, has a similar, shortened variation in the Psalms that is in the plural: "May God grant us grace and bless us, may God's face shine upon us"[1] (Ps. 67:1). But this blessing in Numbers is personal. Let's unpack it.

This blessing is specific. It begins by addressing the physical need. "The LORD bless you and keep you"—it speaks of care (Num. 6:24 NIV). The word *keep* is a specific and tender way God describes His care for us in Scripture. It is a way He describes how faithful He is in His caretaking of us.

Take, for instance, Psalm 121, a passage you may know and love. This psalm has been said to have likely been sung during the pilgrimage of the Jews back to Jerusalem after their exile. The things written in this beautiful psalm were meant to inspire a concrete confidence in the Lord. In it, God is described as Keeper and His people are the "kept."[3]

What are some ways you have felt "kept" or taken care of by God, even in the midst of life being hard or complicated? Have you ever considered this a blessing?

The second part of this blessing in Numbers speaks of God's lavish grace to us. "The LORD make his face shine on you and be gracious to you" (6:25 NIV). The Bible speaks to so many instances of God's grace to us, and His mercy.

What are some ways you have felt God giving you grace and mercy? Have you considered this a blessing?

The third part of this very personal blessing is the most intimate part: "The LORD turn his face toward you and give you peace" (v. 26 NIV). The thought of God turning His face toward us is so precious. It is Him giving us His full attention, and thereby, we gain peace. Even thinking about this right now settles me.

Close your eyes and picture the Lord turning His face toward you. What feelings come up? How does it feel to get the attention of God?

I think we all agree: we want to be blessed by God. Here are a few more promises I feel sure you want:

To be blessed despite hard circumstances:

Blessed are the poor in spirit,
for theirs is the kingdom of heaven.
Blessed are those who mourn,
for they will be comforted.

To be blessed for your unseen character:

Blessed are the meek,
for they will inherit the earth.

To be blessed as you hunger after God:

Blessed are those who hunger and thirst for righteousness,
for they will be filled.

To be blessed for how you extend lavish grace on others:

Blessed are the merciful,
for they will be shown mercy.

To be blessed for your pure heart:

Blessed are the pure in heart,
for they will see God.

To be blessed for your response to turmoil:
Blessed are the peacemakers,
for they will be called children of God.

To be blessed for how you endure unfair treatment for the cause of Christ:
Blessed are those who are persecuted because of righteousness,
for theirs is the kingdom of heaven.

All these blessings from Matthew 5:1–10 (NIV) come from desiring God and putting on His character, and as a by-product, these qualities come out. It is only possible through intimacy with Him. That's where it starts, and these are the outflow.

Write down Matthew 6:33. What is the command here, and how does it support the "first desire, then blessings" principle?

Genesis 1:22–28: This passage describes God's blessing on humanity at creation. He blessed them with fruitfulness, multiplication, dominion over the earth, and the ability to be a blessing to others.

When you seek the kingdom first, you will be humble, you will crave justice, and you will be merciful and pure. You will work for peace. Instead of asking, "How can I work harder to fight for justice?" or "How do I become humbler?" realize that, like blessing, these things will become the natural outflow of a heart pursuing God more than it pursues anything else. Think about it. Have you ever seen a person who wants God more than anything who doesn't also love people well? Who isn't also an incredibly

Psalm 23: This psalm is a beautiful reflection on God's goodness and faithfulness. It describes how God blesses us with provision, guidance, and protection.

Ephesians 1:3–14: This passage describes the spiritual blessings we have received in Christ Jesus. These blessings include forgiveness of sins, adoption into God's family, and the inheritance of eternal life.

humble human being? I'm not talking about a really good theologian or someone who can quote the Bible front to back. I'm talking about character. You can be a moral person without God, but you will never be a true fruit producer without Him. Your passion will be attached to temporary highs from acts of kindness. Your service will ultimately be, in some part, self-serving.

God is a God of blessing, friend. Remember: He loves us. And we want to give beautiful things to those we love. But the litmus test cannot be the material and the physical. And defining or focusing on blessing instead of on God isn't wanting Him most.

DAY 4

What Is in My Way?

What if I told you that you were in your own way of your blessing?

You might have some form of a story like mine, where at one time there was something you thought you wanted—a relationship, a job, a house—and you didn't get it. Then, miles down the road you look back and think, *I'm so glad God did not allow me to have what I thought I wanted.* At the time you might have thought you missed out on a huge blessing—one that God was cruelly withholding from you. Yet the blessing was that God knew better than you did about it. Thank goodness you aren't actually running your own life. If you were, you would have given yourself a much lesser blessing than He did. Or maybe not a blessing at all.

Describe a time when you didn't get the "blessing" you thought you wanted—only to realize later it wouldn't have been a blessing after all. How did God bless you by withholding it? Write down those details. (And then pause and thank the Lord for it!)

Our biggest stumbling block to receiving blessing from God is focusing on lesser blessings and often chasing after them. In doing that we can miss the biggest blessing: God. We miss the purity of just spending time with Him. Getting to know God for who He is and how He wants to be in our lives.

Quite honestly, we don't ask God for *enough*—which, by the way, doesn't mean more stuff. This is a shift for many of us who have spent our lives believing, maybe even been told by a spiritual authority, that we shouldn't ask God for things or on the opposite end, we should pray for endless personal prosperity. Actually, it's not that we are asking God for too much; it's that the things we do ask Him for aren't the things we truly need. This comes into play heavily in the context of blessing.

The peace and joy He wants to give to us are of more worth than every physical blessing we could think to ask of Him.

It's sort of ridiculous if you stop and think about the way we approach this whole blessing thing. It would be like my young adult daughter coming to me and asking me for a pair of my shoes instead of asking for my diamond cocktail ring. Of course I'd give her my forty-dollar shoes. I have plenty of others. They aren't worth nearly as much as my ring. She doesn't realize that I would also gladly give her my ring. She's my daughter. I love her and would do anything for her and give her anything.

But all she wants is something worth much, much less.

God Himself is priceless, so the illustration is a rough comparison. But I think you get the picture. The peace and joy He wants to give to us are of more worth than every physical blessing we could think to ask of Him. But we often settle for asking Him for a house. A car. Some money. Those things are nothing in comparison to contentedness in Him. There's nothing wrong with asking for a house—shelter is a basic need of life. But there's a reason Paul wrote, "Not that I am speaking of being in need, for I have learned, in whatever situation, I am to be content. I know how to be brought low, and I know how to abound. In any and every circumstance, I have learned the secret of facing plenty and hunger, abundance and need" (Phil. 4:11–12 ESV). We must die to the longing for every physical need—yes, even the basic ones—because life is ultimately not about them. It's about finding our pleasure in Christ and trusting Him with our daily provision. I realize this is not an easy job for a selfish human (waving my human hand wildly). But nothing is impossible with the help of the Holy Spirit. We do believe this, yes?

In what way(s) can you apply Paul's testimony to your own life desires?

If you've been thinking about blessings in terms of the physical, how can you shift your focus to asking God for more, not less (more being Him)?

List your top three prayer requests of God below. How can you make the shift to begin praying for more of God in those requests?

Initial Requests	Amended Requests

So yes, our idol can be our small, worldly view of God's blessing ... that small view that can prevent us from seeing how He wants to bless us more than anything else. Other ways we get in our own way:

- **Assumptions/Expectations:** With our limited understanding, we can assume God is doing things He isn't, or not doing things we have no idea about. We can conclude He doesn't love us because He isn't blessing us in the way "they" are blessed. When our blessing isn't the way we expected, we can erroneously think we need to do something to gain God's favor. This can keep us in a constant cycle of behavior modification and good works to please God.

How have your assumptions/expectations prevented you from seeing God's blessings?

- **Limited vision:** When it comes to our faith and recognizing our blessings, our problem is often our limited vision. We may see only what is right in front of us, or what *looks like* a blessing as defined by culture (growth numbers, outside approval, ease of life, etc.) because it is more familiar. This keeps us diminishing—or missing altogether—small acts of faithfulness in lieu of larger-scale but often more surface-level things.

When was a time your vision was limited and because of it you missed seeing a blessing that was right in front of you?

- **Distraction:** We can become distracted by our quest for a blessing—or a specific type of blessing—and then become disappointed when we don't believe God has given it. This tunnel vision for wanting outside of God prevents gratitude for what He is actually giving us, and has given us, and we miss the blessing right in front of us.

What blessing have you missed because of your quest for a *different* blessing?

I don't want to get in my own way. I don't believe it is worth missing out on experiencing the true blessing of God Himself. I don't want to ask God for shoes when I know He would give me a diamond ring.

What about you?

Write a prayer to God sharing the ways you want to exchange the small asks for the bigger way of knowing God more.

DAY 5

How Can I Have a Soul Revival?

We are blessed when we use our mouths to bless God. In this, our souls become revived.

Something happens in our spirits when we bless the Lord. David knew this, and he often used his pen to write praise to the One who blesses us with His very presence, ushering us into it. Isn't it incredible how it works that way? We bless God, and in turn, He blesses us?

I thought it would be good to end this session by meditating on Psalm 103, a psalm we talked about earlier in the week. Wherever you are, if you possibly can, read it aloud. Even better—if you can, go outside and read it. I love being outside with the Lord, speaking to Him in the very nature our Great Creator designed.

> Bless the LORD, O my soul;
> And all that is within me, bless His holy name!
> Bless the LORD, O my soul,
> And forget not all His benefits:
> Who forgives all your iniquities,
> Who heals all your diseases,
> Who redeems your life from destruction,
> Who crowns you with lovingkindness and tender mercies,
> Who satisfies your mouth with good things,
> So that your youth is renewed like the eagle's.

The LORD executes righteousness
And justice for all who are oppressed.
He made known His ways to Moses,
His acts to the children of Israel.
The LORD is merciful and gracious,
Slow to anger, and abounding in mercy.
He will not always strive with us,
Nor will He keep His anger forever.
He has not dealt with us according to our sins,
Nor punished us according to our iniquities.

For as the heavens are high above the earth,
So great is His mercy toward those who fear Him;
As far as the east is from the west,
So far has He removed our transgressions from us.
As a father pities his children,
So the LORD pities those who fear Him.
For He knows our frame;
He remembers that we are dust.

As for man, his days are like grass;
As a flower of the field, so he flourishes.
For the wind passes over it, and it is gone,
And its place remembers it no more.
But the mercy of the LORD is from everlasting to everlasting
On those who fear Him,
And His righteousness to children's children,
To such as keep His covenant,
And to those who remember His commandments to do them.
The LORD has established His throne in heaven,
And His kingdom rules over all.

Bless the LORD, you His angels,
Who excel in strength, who do His word,
Heeding the voice of His word.
Bless the LORD, all you His hosts,
You ministers of His, who do His pleasure.
Bless the LORD, all His works,
In all places of His dominion.

Bless the LORD, O my soul! (NKJV)

It's hard to think about wanting more "things" when our mouths are full of blessing God! I don't know about you, but I feel blessed to just praise Him right now.

Practicing Soul Revival

Let's get right to it and dive into our revival formula from Revelation 2 in the context of blessing:

REMEMBER

Remembrance is an especially powerful practice for us as we think of blessing. It puts us in a mode of gratitude, which is so important. The most significant historical events—Jesus' death and resurrection, which are the ultimate blessings—should remind us that if He never blessed us with another thing, for us that is enough.

How does remembering the cross change the idea of blessing for you? How might your daily life and habits reflect this belief?

Read Psalm 104. **Write down the blessings of who God is in the context of all He has done as you read this incredible passage (a favorite of mine!).**

REPENT

Confess to God all the ways you've desired physical blessings over just Him ... the assumptions or expectations that you've placed on Him ... the ways you've used Him as your personal genie or vending machine. Ask Him to forgive you for the ways you've confused and desired His blessing more than Him, and ask for His help to see the incredible blessing in just soaking up who He is.

Write down a prayer of confession and of blessing for God.

REPEAT

This week, we talked about how our habit of seeking tangible blessings keeps us focused on wanting blessing more than we want God. These are my top three suggestions for changing this mindset:

1. Pray.
2. Read the Bible regularly.
3. Place yourself where you can see God's transformative work by serving somewhere that stretches you (volunteer, lead a small group, participate in jail ministry, etc.). You will walk away experiencing God with a new understanding of the concept of blessing.

What is one spiritual discipline you have that helps you want God most?

What is at least one daily spiritual habit you want to develop to increase your desire to want God most?

Reflect on your week. How might you remember, repent, and repeat this week, focusing on desiring God more than you desire His blessing?

Remember	Repent	Repeat

Session 6

COMING BACK

RETURN TO THE LORD YOUR GOD, FOR HE IS MERCIFUL AND COMPASSIONATE.

Joel 2:13b

Memorize this verse this week by our repetition model.

To follow along in the *I Want God* book, read chapter 12.

DAY 1

Video and Outline

Stream the "Coming Back to God" (session 6) video (link on p. 17) and complete the session 6 outline below as you watch.

Group leaders: See the session 6 guide in the back (p. 198) for group discussion information.

- **There's only been one ____________________, and it's ____________________.**
- **In His kindness, God was willing to restore them if they would return to Him in ____________________.**
  It's the same grace He is willing to extend to us today, no matter our ____________________.
- **This is a huge theme with the Lord—from Genesis to Revelation, from the Israelites to the church at Ephesus—always a call to return to Him with ____________________.**
- **This is not about mustering up a burst of ____________________ for a comeback. It is bringing your ____________________**

____________________ and saying, "I'm here, wanting to love You most. May I come back?"

✦ The prodigal son wanted freedom. But, ultimately, he wanted what we all want: ____________________.

✦ Most of us don't really know what we want in life because we have settled for so long for ____________________. So we are quick to walk away from our ____________________, Jesus.

✦ No matter what has been in the way, it's not ____________________. Too many times, we think we have to stay somewhere because it's what we know, but that's not biblical. It is counter to a God who says, "See, I am doing a ____________________! Now it springs up; do you not perceive it? I am making a way in the wilderness and streams in the wasteland" (Isa. 43:19 NIV).

✦ The truth is:

- You are never ____________________.
- You can always ____________________.
- You can forever ____________________.

✦ You will never regret ____________________. There will never be anything worth more than giving your entire life to Jesus Christ, the great Lover of your soul.

✦ Remember Him forever. Repent often. Repeat the ____________________ that draw you closer to ____________________ every day for the rest of your life.

DAY 2

What Is My Real Issue?

You and Jesus. Your one great love story. That is what this is all about.

It is about His coming to die for you, the consequence of that death and His resurrection, and your commitment back to Him by accepting that inconceivable free gift and the life it offers. It is about your walking away at times in this relationship and His pursuit of you to come back. Maybe that time is right now, maybe it has been a time in your past, or maybe it will be a time in your future.

Along the way, there have likely been other loves. Ones that asked for your time and attention. Ones that have felt more easily attainable, and subsequently, immediately enjoyable. Perhaps they have promised big, and they might have even temporarily delivered. But in the end, there will always and only be the One your soul truly desires: Jesus.

That is the real issue.

Journal some of the highs and lows of your life on the timeline below and on the following pages. On it list things like walking away from God, coming back, pivotal moments, and so on.

Now looking back, how has your love story with Jesus affected your life story?

I fell hard for Jesus when I was six. I will never forget it. I was born into life in the church and all things the Lord, so I never really knew life apart from Him. My parents introduced me to Jesus. I'd learned of Him in church and Sunday school. And yet, there came that moment when I wanted Him, not just to know about Him.

It was a Sunday night, and our church in Oklahoma was having what they used to call a "passion play," where people in the church would act out scenes from the Bible in some costumes we assumed looked like clothes from the Bible days. If you're not familiar with passion plays, they might sound weird. But for me, not only were they perfectly normal, they were something

I came to love and hold as a dear church tradition. The casting of these plays started with the choir, since the plays would involve musical numbers. The lead actors were often the best singers in the church. Church folks of all ages—young and old—made up the people in the crowds … the ones waving palm branches for Jesus' arrival on a donkey (yes, we got a real donkey, and it would really walk down the center aisle of the church) … the ones shouting, "Crucify Him!" during the intense crucifixion scene. The character of Jesus was always played by someone bearded, but that was about as close as anyone knew to what Jesus looked like. (True story: One time a church I attended got desperate for a Jesus and at the last minute, recruited a man who worked at the local Subway to play Him!)

I dearly loved watching these plays, and I well remember how I felt watching the play that Sunday night when I was six. I was overwhelmed by my desire for this Jesus I saw being portrayed in front of me. All the stories I had learned in VBS … the stories my mother had read to me from the big white coffee-table Bible at night … the stories my father would preach from the pulpit on Sunday morning … suddenly they were being acted out in front of me and coming to life. There was something about seeing them. (Like watching *The Chosen* for so many of us!) In those moments of watching the stories unfold in front of me, something clicked in my heart to make it *personal*. I invited Jesus to come inside my heart and soul. And He did.

I wish our love story had just taken off from there, without any complications—that in the now forty-five years I've been a believer, I'd never needed to come back because I'd never gone anywhere to need to return from. But that is not my story and is likely not yours.

MY LIFE'S JOURNEY (cont.)

What is true is that many times I've had to come back. Many times, I've loved other people (and things) more than I loved Jesus. Some of those times that person has been me. I grieve that, but I must also be honest about it. What about you?

What has it looked like in your life to need to come back to the Lord? Are you at a place that you need to come back right now?

We have been talking for six sessions about identifying our idols so we can want God with an all-in heart because admitting these things is important to your love story. That's why we are returning to it again in this moment. In every session, we have plugged in our revival formula from Revelation 2 (remember, repent, repeat), looking at it in the specific context of each subject we were studying, because it is a practice worth repeating. The reason? To help us renew our passion for the Lord so we can experience true revival.

We often talk about revival in the church as if it's some unattainable happening, as if God is looking down from heaven and there's a bit of luck and favoritism to where revival falls. We think, *Maybe it won't come to us*, or *Maybe we won't be chosen for it*, or *Maybe we can mimic it.*

We think it's solely a corporate gathering, so if we miss a revival night at our church, we will miss experiencing God.

This is not about mustering up a burst of spiritual energy for a comeback. It is quite literally bringing your exhausted soul to the Lord and saying, *I'm here, wanting to love You most. May I come back?*

I want to say very clearly that God can indeed do what He wants when He wants, and no one can force the Holy Spirit to bring revival. But there is a reason posture and positioning are critical in this process, because revival is not about drawing a "lucky number" to receive the prize. And it's not about God choosing a favorite church to bring it to. By the time we see a corporate revival, there have already been individual things happening. It's personal—with God. It's always been personal. Heart rending. Position of surrender. Posture of repentance. Coming back is about intimacy with Him. And it can happen anytime, anywhere. It's all about seeking the Lord for ourselves as we recognize our need for Him. This *can* happen in a church setting. It can also happen on the floor of your bathroom, alone with the Lord.

"God may want to do something amazing around you, but first He wants to do it *in you*."[1]

How and where do you need God in your life right now? How are you reaching for other things instead of pursuing Him in that need?

Our memory verse in this session is from Joel 2, and it's such an important chapter in the Bible—for multiple reasons. Here are verses 12–13:

> "Even now," declares the LORD,
> "return to me with all your heart,
> with fasting and weeping and mourning."
>
> Rend your heart
> and not your garments.
> Return to the LORD your God,
> for he is gracious and compassionate,
> slow to anger and abounding in love,
> and he relents from sending calamity. (NIV)

In this chapter is an important message of "come back" if I've ever heard one. Joel is imploring Judah to return to the Lord and addressing the infestation of locusts that resulted from their sin and waywardness. So often the famous verse "I will repay you for the years the locusts have eaten" (v. 25a NIV) is misinterpreted to suggest that God is going to honor what other people or circumstances have taken from us. In context, God was talking about the pain that Judah had in fact brought upon themselves due to their own sin. In His kindness, God was willing to restore them if they would return to Him in repentance and faithfulness. It is the same grace He is willing to extend to us today.

He extended this same grace to the Ephesian church when He said, "Turn back to me" (Rev. 2:5).

I don't know what you've been taught or if you've felt shame in coming back to God. Maybe you've thought, *I've done this too many times ... God must be sick of me confessing, then messing up again.* Or maybe you're just feeling unworthy or tired at the moment. But this is not about mustering up a burst of spiritual energy for a comeback. It is quite literally bringing your exhausted soul to the Lord and saying, *I'm here, wanting to love You most. May I come back?*

Watch Him open His arms and welcome you in.

How much do you need to feel the welcoming arms of the Lord holding you right now? Write down a prayer of complete abandon in your weariness and wanting. Ask Him to hold you. He is faithful and willing.

DAY 3

What Do I Want?

The prodigal son in Luke 15 wanted freedom. But ultimately, he wanted acceptance and love.

Many times, when we find ourselves wandering, we want things that feel urgent, which causes us to pursue them with urgency. If you read that to mean foolishly and recklessly at times, that is exactly what I mean, as well. Our urgency will have us acting out in all kinds of detrimental ways. Watch a person determined to cover up sin, and you'll be watching an utter fool. Watch a person determined to numb a feeling of pain, and you'll be watching a person without regard for safety, respect, or dignity—hers or yours.

Write about a time you pursued something that felt like an urgent want or need, and you acted foolishly in your pursuit of it. (Or a time you recall someone close to you doing this.) What were some of the ramifications of that pursuit?

Back to the prodigal son.

It's always struck me that he didn't really know what he wanted when he left home. This is often the case for us, which is perhaps why Jesus questioned, "What do you want?" in John 1.

So many times, we don't even know. We are not equipped to know. We do a lot of inaccurate guessing and searching.

Am I hungry? *Let me satisfy my hunger pangs with food.* (Esau)

Do I crave freedom? *Let me run off with my money and try to find it in indulgence.* (the prodigal)

Am I able to control this situation? *Let me make everything perfect.* (Martha)

In each of these cases, the actual want was to fill some ache inside, the God ache.

Describe a time when you suspect what you were looking for wasn't your actual need? Write about that.

We will feel constant conflict: between the flesh we want to please and the heart we have for home.

I don't want us to do any more guessing or searching.

What we want is God. There is a desire that He put within us meant only for Him. There is, too, a desire to come back to Him when we are far from Him. It is why we begin to feel inward pain when we run away from where our hearts are at home. It is not the way it is meant to be, and we know it. We will feel constant conflict: between the flesh we want to please and the heart we have for home.

We can stop the guessing with a good process.

1. **Desire.** The fact that you want to want God is a start. You are doing this study, so that shows a desire for Him!
2. **Choice.** Remember the principle of the greater desire? That's the choice for what you want most.
3. **Support.** Live in a way that backs up the choice you make and what you're committed to.

I also don't want us making choices to have an all-in heart for God that we don't follow through with. That's the kind of lifestyle that makes you need a comeback. It's one thing to feel passion for the Lord again in the moments after doing a six-week Bible study. It's another to commit to go live your life in the day-to-day after this study is long over. And what you do once that happens is what really matters. Think about it ... plan for it ... because "passion without preparation is a good intention designed to fade."[1]

DAY 4

What Is in My Way?

The dread of coming home late from a date in high school. I can still vividly picture what that looked like and remember many of the emotions. The truth is, the thought of facing my father made me not want to go home.

I didn't typically break curfew—after all, my father was pretty strict when it came to my dating. (I don't think he trusted boys since he once was one!) But I often skated in just in the nick of time, and one time I didn't make it. From my date's car in front of my house, I could see my dad sitting in his chair with the light off behind him, and only the glow of the table lamp beside him lighting up his face. I can still picture it: his large arms and hands holding the sides of the chair, making him look like a giant. I was late, and he was waiting up for me. He wanted to make sure my date saw him and felt properly intimidated. I knew *I did*. I was certain I was in deep trouble. I don't remember my punishment, but really, the lamp/chair/mad-dad scene was punishment enough. I never wanted to be late again.

This type of scene was good for behavior modification. (I wasn't late again!) But it didn't do anything to change my heart about my behavior. I understood that beneath my father's sternness was concern, but my own guilt feelings and the lack of real depth of conversation with him about the why behind his anger just made me feel like a bad daughter. (Like a lot of dads back then, he did the best he knew to do!) My own shame told me that clearly, I *was* bad.

Often, we don't want to approach God because of similar mindsets—shaming from Satan that plays in our minds. Maybe we have strayed from God, done wrong, or just don't feel up to par spiritually, and for reasons like these, we stay away. Maybe our lives have been about behavior modification rather than true heart change, so we haven't experienced the real thing when it comes to a desire to be different. The distance between us and God remains because we are intimidated to come back to Him, feeling like a failure. We feel as if we are a disappointment and He may be mad at us. *What if He won't take me back? What if I am too far gone? What if this time I've really done it and He just won't accept me?*

Have you ever felt intimidated to come back to God? How did that get in your way of returning to Him in love and vulnerability?

Idolatry doesn't have to be ugly. It may look reasonable and even beautiful to us. Those are the sneakiest types of idols. What if your idol is trusting yourself more than you trust God in situations like this one? Because you believe you are too far gone, you trust that your resolve to stay gone is reasonable even though you know the truth from God's Word that He is faithful to welcome you back.

And not believing you *can* come back to God is, in essence, the idol of fear. It is also the idol of disbelief. These things will get in your way of wanting and loving God most.

Has fear or disbelief ever kept you from coming back to God? Write about that.

What scares you most about wanting God over everything else?

What scares you most about giving up your idols?

- **Pride** can also be an idol in your way of coming back to God. Maybe you don't think you need God that much. Perhaps you feel like you've done pretty well on your own, without Him. When we feel adequate, God is not necessary. We are people in desperate need of Him, but that doesn't mean we think we need Him.

Has pride ever kept you from coming back to God? Write about that.

- **Apathy** can be an idol in your way of coming back to God. You can become quite settled in your mode of operation—living apart from God and barely noticing it anymore. Spiritual numbness might be the scariest, darkest place to be. That's a stubborn thing to fix. When we get to the place that we don't even really see God anymore, that's when we most need to fall to our knees and ask Him to shake things up, regardless of what may break loose.

Has apathy ever kept you from coming back to God? Write about that.

- **People** can be an idol in your way of coming back to God. When someone becomes the comfort you need from God—always there to help you, comfort you, advise you, lead you—the one you talk to and always turn to about everything ... then you feel less of a need for the Lord. People can truly get in the way of how God wants to work in you. Relationships are meant to be wonderful and to enrich our lives, but they aren't meant to take the place of God in any way.

Have relationships with people ever kept you from coming back to God? Write about that.

No matter what has been in the way, it's not the end of the story. Too many times we think we have to stay in disbelief, stay in pride (self-sufficiency), stay in apathy, stay in dependency on others, because it is what we *know*. But that's not even biblical. It's counter to a God who says, "See, I am doing a new thing! Now it springs up; do you not perceive it? I am making a way in the wilderness and streams in the wasteland" (Isa. 43:19 NIV).

You are never too far gone.

You can always change.

You can forever come back.

Write an honest prayer sharing how you feel about coming back. Name your emotions in this moment. Confess to God anything you sense Him asking you to release that has been standing in the way of your closeness. Even in this moment, how do you feel as you write out this prayer?

DAY 5

How Can I Have a Soul Revival?

Revival is a work God does in us, but we have choices to make. What choices do you need to make to partner with God in revival?

Let's recall that church in Ephesus we looked at in session 1: the good church people who had forgotten their first love and moved away from Him. God's intention toward them was to bring them back and revive them. But they had to make choices to come back to Him ... in remembrance, repentance, and continual repetition of the good inward works they had done when they fell in love with Him in the beginning.

It is the same for me and you.

We cannot expect to have a vibrant relationship with the Lord without a heart for Him.

We cannot have a halfway heart for Him, but an all-in heart.

We often don't know what we need, and our need is misplaced. But even knowing what we need will not be enough. What is true, no matter what, is we have a place inside us that will always desire God—no matter what other, lesser desires we pursue—and it will never go away.

Practicing Soul Revival

For the last time in this study, let's plug in our revival formula from Revelation 2 in the context of coming back ...

REMEMBER

Whether you are doing this study in crisis or in peace, whether you are far from God and need to come back or you feel close to Him, remembering God is an important practice toward wanting Him more. How will you do this? What will you do to remember God in the moments when you aren't in crisis or far from Him?

> "Our moving away from God causes our eyes to be blinded to the things He is doing. Our minds feel entitled to the things He will do. Our hearts are calloused to the things He has already done. It leaves us vacant and waffling and so grossly unfulfilled."[1]

Forgetfulness affects our past, present, and future. When we forget about the goodness of God, we simply cannot see the present things He is doing in our lives. We may not only overlook our own daily blessings, but we may envy the blessings of others. We can become entitled, thinking we deserve things in the future. And then, when God does not give them to us the way we think He should, we become convinced He is unfaithful. Perhaps most surprising is how it affects our memory of how good God has been to us in the past. Forgetfulness causes us to become callous to the goodness of God in immeasurable ways in our personal histories.

Create a practical remembrance of God.

- **Choose a visual representation from the following ideas:**
  - **a ring, bracelet, or some other jewelry**
  - **a stone in your yard or in a jar**

a note card on your bathroom mirror
a print to hang on your wall or sit on your desk

Why did you choose this representation? How does this visual piece remind you of God? What is the significance?

- Make a Jesus memory book or box: Create this remembrance by filling it with your Jesus story. Continue to add mementos, such as quotes, notes, or anything that reminds you to want God most.

REPENT

Remember: *Repentance* is a serious word, but it is not a scary word. It means a beautiful coming back together. We sin; we must then reconcile.

As you look back over our six weeks together, what do you feel you most need to repent of?

Consider telling a friend about this repentance. Ask her to hold you accountable as you live and pray toward wanting God most.

REPEAT

How will you guard against moving away from God in the future? Don't let your business or your working "for God" draw you away from Him. Remember that the church at Ephesus was busy being good, but they forgot the all-important aspect of a vibrant relationship with God. If we want more of God, we have to take this step of moving forward, which is going back and doing what we did at first.

Look back at session 1: What was your relationship with God like at first?

What did you do at first?

How has your relationship with God changed and grown? Describe it.

If you've grown in your relationship during these six weeks (which is my prayer!), how will you continue repeating the habits you've been growing in?

What is it like now, wanting God more?

Have you come back?

For one final time ... reflect on your week. How might you remember, repent, and repeat this week?

Remember	Repent	Repeat

What does a life look like that remembers, repents, and repeats? How will you hold this tight as you move forward?

As We Close Out This Study

I just want to say I'm so proud of you. I'm with you as we continue to pursue God together. I hope you have truly felt the presence of God during this study, maybe for the first time, or perhaps like never before. You will never regret coming back to God. One thing is sure: He is always waiting for you.

There will never be anything more worth giving your life to than Jesus Christ, the great Lover of your soul. May you remember Him forever. May you repent often. May you repeat the practices that draw you closer to His heart every day for the rest of your life.

I am praying and believing God for revival. Our world needs it. Our families need it. Each of our hearts need it, most of all. May this study have been a small spark for that revival inside your own heart and soul.

That all who see Him through you will watch your life and say, "Whatever she has, I want it."

I love you. Let's go.

Lisa

Leader's Guide

Session 1: Revival

Discussion Starter

After gathering, help your group get acquainted using the following points.

- Get the group started with questions like these: "We're just getting started on this topic, and some people here might be new to each other, but let's dive right in! What made you want to do this particular study?" (Find out if anyone wants specific questions answered.) "Why are you here? What about this topic attracted you?"
- To understand what most people think about the idea of revival, ask studiers to share if they have ever attended a revival or studied any revivals from history. What's their personal experience with or understanding of them? (This study is great for both veteran studiers and new believers, since many won't be familiar with revivals of old, so it will feel like an even playing field.)
- Invite discussion about what everyone hopes to take away at the completion of the study. Ask studiers to write down their answers somewhere to look back on later.

Read Psalm 142:5 as an introduction to the idea of desiring God. Then ask:

- "What have you always thought about the idea of wanting God versus needing God?"
- "How do you think wanting God affects your daily life?"

Watch the session 1 video. Use this completed outline to guide your discussion time.

- ✦ **Revivals are incredible moves of God.**
- ✦ **Revivals start inside the soul of a someone who is coming to God for the first time or coming back to God with a ready and contrite heart.**
- ✦ **Revival isn't just about a corporate gathering. It's about what God does to bring you back to life.**
- ✦ **Desperation is often the exact right positioning to be in to bring on needed revival.**
- ✦ **Cycle of longing:**

  1. **We have a longing for something.**
  2. **We act on the longing.**
  3. **We experience often temporary results that satisfy the longing.**
  4. **We still long and either change our longing to something else … or change our method of getting the same longing in our persistence.**

- ✦ **Jesus Himself asked the very question "What do you want?" in John 1—a question that went straight to longing.**
- ✦ **The word that is repeated three times in this passage (Matt. 22:37), *ALL*, tells us what kind of heart God wants. It's also the kind of life God wants from us and for us: the all-in life.**
- ✦ **If we don't want God the most, if He's not our primary longing, then today can start a new positioning: a heart that is postured and ready for revival.**

- **The benefit of knowing what you want: the complications of daily life decisions become a lot clearer and less complicated.**

- **A good way to know if something has become an idol in your life is to ask yourself these questions:**

    1. **Do I try hard to keep something and will I think of creative ways to keep it?**
    2. **Do I not tell people the full truth about the hold it has on me?**
    3. **Do I grieve letting it go?**

- **God may want to do something around us, but first He wants to do something in us.**

Ask a few questions from the session as time allows.
Close your time in prayer.

Session 2: More Than Comfort

Discussion Starter

After gathering and getting settled in, discuss the following points.

- Ask: "What comes to mind when you think of the word *comfort*?" Take only a few minutes to share responses.
- Ask studiers to share a favorite story from Scripture about when God comforted someone.
- Then ask the group to share their own personal stories about a time they sought to comfort themselves versus a time God comforted them. (Talk about the differences.)

Read Romans 2:4. (I recommend *The Message* paraphrase, which can be found online at sites like BibleGateway.com.)

- Invite discussion about how God calling us to more often disrupts our comfort but is for our good.
- Touch on the story of Jacob and Esau in Genesis 25. Discuss how, in the end, Esau's desire for human comfort (in the form of food) cost him what he really wanted, and how we relate to that.

Watch the session 2 video. Use this completed outline to guide your discussion time.

- **The idol of comfort might be what is stopping you from experiencing lasting, deep, and true revival.**
- **Everything has a cost. We just don't always think about that at the time we are enjoying a temporary solution.**
- **Comfort in and of itself is not an idol. God Himself is our great comforter, and He desires that we bring our burdens to Him so He can properly comfort us.**
- **We turn comfort into an idol when we elevate it. The problem comes in when we try to comfort ourselves through temporary measures instead of Christ.**
- **Comfort presents like the best friend you will ever have, but in the process of "comforting" you, it robs what you really want in life right out from under you.**
- **What comfort really does to you:**
    - **It affects your relationships with others.**
    - **It affects your relationship with yourself.**
    - **It affects your relationship with God.**
- **When God allows discomfort in our lives, He does us the biggest favor we never wanted.**
- **Taking comfort into our own hands gets in our way because it keeps us from:**
    1. **Knowing who we really are.**
    2. **Living in freedom with a healthy perspective.**
    3. **Enjoying our full potential for Christ.**

- **God will always be the true and lasting comfort we need in the midst of this difficult life.**

- **As you seek to have revival in this area of your life and come back to God, remember who He is as the great comforter, repent from that comfort idol that's gotten in your way, and repeat that continual seeking of Him to bring you what you need to soothe and relieve your weary soul.**

Ask a few questions from the session as time allows.

Close your time in prayer.

Session 3: More Than Control

Discussion Starter

After gathering and getting settled in, discuss the following points.

- Ask: "What is your response to the word *control*?" Take only a few minutes to share responses.
- Ask studiers to share a favorite story from Scripture about when someone tried to control the hand of God. How did it turn out?
- Then ask: "In what way(s) have you ever tried to control God?" Encourage studiers to be honest as they share. Be ready to lead by going first. (Think about the when—wanting God to do things on your timetable; the what—wanting God to do what we want and being frustrated when He doesn't; the how—we pray and say, "God, I will do this if You will do that …")

Read John 16:33.

- Discuss what this verse tells us about control and what part of life is up to us and what is up to God.

Watch the session 3 video. Use this completed outline to guide your discussion time.

- With all the hardship of this world, the goodness of God doesn't always make logical sense.
- We want God to make sense to us so that we can have some type of control over what is happening around us that we do not understand.
- It's the pull of control in us that presents in subtle ways through our frustration and even disillusionment that causes us to ask, Why isn't God doing what we want?
- Coming back to God is sometimes surrendering what you've been trying to control.
- When God seems to not make sense and things are out of our control, we can start to do one of these things:
    1. We can doubt.
    2. We can become angry.
    3. We can try to take matters into our own hands.
- We think controlling is the way, but in the end, control:
    - Exhausts us.
    - Leads to disillusionment.
    - Creates distance from God.
- The principle of the greater desire: forgoing what you want in the moment for what you want most.
- Fear and control are closely connected.
- When the Lord says, "Fear not," in places like Isaiah 41:10, He is not just calling us to release our fears to Him; He is also calling us to surrender our control. Think about it like Him also saying, "Control not."
- We can know we are learning to trust God more when we see ourselves trying to control our circumstances less.

- ✦ **Prayer is the action we need when we feel afraid.**
- ✦ **We know of God's great overcoming of this world, even as we live in a world that often doesn't appear to be in any control. God assured us of this for one purpose: so that in Him we might have peace.**

Ask a few questions from the session as time allows.

Close your time in prayer.

Session 4: More Than Popularity

Discussion Starter

After gathering and getting settled in, discuss the following points.

- Ask: "What is your response to the word *popularity*?" Take only a few minutes to share responses.
- Ask studiers to share a favorite story from Scripture about when someone's behavior was more about pleasing others than about obeying God. How did it turn out?
- Then ask them to share their own stories with people-pleasing and seeking approval or popularity. Encourage studiers to look beyond a high school definition of *popularity* and think about ways the approval of man affects their lives today, perhaps in even greater measure (for example, being unwilling to speak up for Christ, not wanting to witness, overextending your schedule, and so on). Ask for honesty as they share. Be ready to lead by going first.

Read Galatians 1:10. (I recommend the CEV translation, which can be found online at sites like BibleGateway.com.)

- Discuss how Paul was saying in this verse that pleasing man is "off mission," how that affects us, and one way this week to get back on course.

Watch the session 4 video. Use this completed outline to guide your discussion time.

- ✦ The idol of popularity is really about wanting approval by others.
- ✦ There is a cycle of popularity that happens:
    - We want to be popular ▶ which creates motives ▶ which dictates our actions ▶ so we live as people-pleasers.
- ✦ Here's how popularity (aka, the approval of man, people-pleasing) affects us:
    1. It changes what we want and will fight for.
    2. It changes the convictions we are willing to hold and the conversations we are willing to have.
    3. It changes our dependence on God and can form pride within us.
- ✦ John 12:43 sums it all up well when he writes of the Pharisees: "They loved human praise more than the praise of God."
- ✦ We crave these things:
    1. Acceptance: to feel part of something important, part of a group, part of a family
    2. Unconditional love: to be loved for who we are, fully, completely, without strings, parameters, or conditions
    3. Being known: to be recognized in our uniqueness, thoroughly understood
    4. Significance: to leave a legacy and feel as though we matter
- ✦ It's not wrong to want to be accepted, known, significant, or unconditionally loved, but when we want it so much we are willing to seek those things by means other than God, we take matters into our own hands and it often goes wrong.
- ✦ The one who is worthy of your soul's desire is the one who knows you and loves you most.

Ask a few questions from the session as time allows.

Close your time in prayer.

Session 5: More Than Blessing

Discussion Starter

After gathering and getting settled in, discuss the following points.

- Ask: "What is your definition of the word *blessing*?" Take only a few minutes to share responses.
- Ask studiers to share a favorite story from Scripture about when someone was blessed by God and what this looked like. Was the blessing what the world might expect?
- Then ask them to share their own stories of blessing in their lives. Did they feel God has blessed them, and how? Did they ever feel He has blessed others at times and bypassed them, and what made them think or feel that way? Listen as they share, and withhold judgment or overly spiritual quick responses. Be ready to lead by going first.

Read Ephesians 1:3.

- Discuss what this verse means, particularly the phrase "who has blessed us in Christ with every spiritual blessing in the heavenly places" (ESV).

Watch the session 5 video. Use this completed outline to guide your discussion time.

✦ **The way we see** blessing **is tied to the way we** experience the blessings **in our lives.**

✦ **A right view of blessing:**

1. **It comes from** spiritual maturity**.**
2. **It's rooted in** the Bible**.**

3. Blessing is ultimately for heaven, not for earth.
4. Blessing is directly tied to the benefits of God Himself.

- ✦ Sometimes the reason we don't feel blessed is because we can't see it.
- ✦ Not feeling blessed is often due to our perspective rather than our reality. This can be because of one or more of these things:

1. Assumptions/Expectations
2. Limited Vision
3. Distraction

- ✦ When it comes to blessing, we have a skewed understanding of what it is and how God wants to bless us in the supernatural versus the natural.
- ✦ As a result of skewed understanding, we form a transactional relationship with God, which has two negative effects:

1. It becomes or stays very self-focused. (As we center on how we can get more, we become more and more inward focused. The result = pride.)
2. It robs us of real depth with the Lord, and in the end, we miss true blessings. (When we misunderstand true blessings, we may miss the package[s] they come in that we are not expecting. The result = disappointment and a lack of true joy.)

- ✦ We've all had times when we've settled for a transactional relationship with the Lord, but God is ready and waiting for us to see Him for the blessing He is and come back to the purity of just wanting Him.

Ask a few questions from the session as time allows.

Close your time in prayer.

Session 6: Coming Back

Discussion Starter

After gathering and getting settled in, discuss the following points.

- Ask: "What comes to mind when someone talks about the word *comeback*?" Take only a few minutes to share responses.
- Ask: "What is your definition of the word *repentance*?"
- Discuss what it would mean to consider a comeback in the idea of "coming back together" with the Lord through the act of repentance. How might that change the way your group looked at the world's definition of a comeback?

Read Joel 2:13.

- Discuss how the mercy and compassion of the Lord in our returning to Him changes our willingness to come back to Him and how He's different from any human we have been distant from.

Watch the session 6 video. Use this completed outline to guide your discussion time.

✦ **There's only been one true lover of your soul, and it's Jesus Christ.**

✦ **In His kindness, God was willing to restore them if they would return to Him in repentance and faithfulness. It's the same grace He is willing to extend to us today, no matter our circumstances.**

✦ **This is a huge theme with the Lord—from Genesis to Revelation, from the Israelites to the church at Ephesus—always a call to return to Him with grace and love and acceptance.**

✦ **This is not about mustering up a burst of spiritual energy for a comeback. It is bringing your exhausted soul to the Lord and saying, "I'm here, wanting to love You most. May I come back?"**

- ✦ The prodigal son wanted freedom. But, ultimately, he wanted what we all want: acceptance and love.
- ✦ Most of us don't really know what we want in life because we have settled for so long for lesser loves. So we are quick to walk away from our real love, Jesus.
- ✦ No matter what has been in the way, it's not the end of the story. Too many times, we think we have to stay somewhere because it's what we know, but that's not biblical. It is counter to a God who says, "See, I am doing a new thing! Now it springs up; do you not perceive it? I am making a way in the wilderness and streams in the wasteland" (Isa. 43:19 NIV).
- ✦ The truth is:
    - You are never too far gone.
    - You can always change.
    - You can forever come back.
- ✦ You will never regret giving Jesus everything. There will never be anything worth more than giving your entire life to Jesus Christ, the great Lover of your soul.
- ✦ Remember Him forever. Repent often. Repeat the practices that draw you closer to His heart every day for the rest of your life.

Ask a few questions from the session as time allows.

Close your time in prayer.

Notes

Session 1, Day 3

1. D. A. Carson, *The Gospel according to John, The Pillar New Testament Commentary* (Grand Rapids, MI: Eerdmans, 1991), 154–55.

2. Augustine of Hippo, *Confessions*, 1,1.5, quoted in The Holy See, accessed April 12, 2024, www.vatican.va/spirit/documents/spirit_20020821_agostino_en.html.

3. Lisa Whittle, *I Want God: How to Love Him with Your Whole Heart and Revive Your Soul* (Nashville, TN: W Publishing, 2024), 154.

Session 1, Day 4

1. Blaise Pascal, *Pensées* (New York: Penguin Books, 1966), 75.

2. Tim Keller, *Counterfeit Gods: The Empty Promises of Money, Sex, and Power, and the Only Hope That Matters*, repr. ed. (New York: Penguin, 2016), xvii.

Session 1, Day 5

1. Whittle, *I Want God*, 23–24.

2. Drawn from Whittle, *I Want God*, 149–60.

3. David Seal, "Revelation, Book of," in *The Lexham Bible Dictionary*, ed. John D. Barry et al. (Bellingham, WA: Lexham, 2016), Logos Bible Study app, accessed February 15, 2024.

4. Michele Cushatt, *Undone: A Story of Making Peace with an Unexpected Life* (Grand Rapids, MI: Zondervan, 2015), 22.

Session 2, Day 3

1. Lisa Whittle, *I Want God: How to Love Him with Your Whole Heart and Revive Your Soul* (Nashville, TN: W Publishing, 2024), 56.

2. Whittle, *I Want God*, 27.

3. Whittle, *I Want God*, 61–62.

Session 2, Day 4

1. Pamela J. Scalise, "Haggai, Book of," in *The Lexham Bible Dictionary*, ed. John D. Barry et al. (Bellingham, WA: Lexham Press, 2016), Logos Bible Study app, accessed February 15, 2024.

2. Whittle, *I Want God*, 57.

3. John D. Barry et al., eds., "Birthright," in *The Lexham Bible Dictionary* (Bellingham, WA: Lexham Press, 2016), Logos Bible Study app, accessed February 15, 2024.

4. F. F. Bruce et al., *The Origin of the Bible*, ed. Philip W. Comfort, enl. and rev. ed. (Carol Stream, IL: Tyndale, 2020), 262–63.

Session 2, Day 5

1. Elisabeth Elliot, *Passion and Purity* (Grand Rapids, MI: Revell, 2002), 90.

2. Lisa Whittle, *The Hard Good: Showing Up for God to Work in You When You Want to Shut Down* (Nashville, TN: Thomas Nelson, 2021).

Session 3, Day 2

1. Anna Whiston-Donaldson, *Rare Bird: A Memoir of Loss and Love* (New York: Convergent, 2015).

Session 3, Day 4

1. Oswald Chambers, *My Utmost for His Highest*, ed. Macy Halford (Grand Rapids, MI: Our Daily Bread), January 22, 132.

Session 3, Day 5

1. Lisa Whittle, *I Want God: How to Love Him with Your Whole Heart and Revive Your Soul* (Nashville, TN: W Publishing, 2024), 89.

Session 4, Day 3

1. Lisa Whittle, *Jesus over Everything Bible Study Guide* (Nashville, TN: HarperChristian Resources, 2020), 35.

Session 4, Day 5

1. Lisa Whittle, *I Want God: How to Love Him with Your Whole Heart and Revive Your Soul* (Nashville, TN: W Publishing, 2024), 102.

Session 5, Day 3

1. Amy Flattery, "The Significance of the Priestly Blessing," AG News, July 11, 2023, https://news.ag.org/en/article-repository/spiritual-life/2023/07/the-significance-of-the-priestly-blessing.

2. Flattery, "The Significance of the Priestly Blessing."

3. David Blynov, "The Lord as Keeper," Medium, June 14, 2023, https://medium.com/@davidblynov/the-lord-as-keeper-b853f9200d42#:.

Session 6, Day 2

1. Lisa Whittle, *I Want God: How to Love Him with Your Whole Heart and Revive Your Soul* (Nashville, TN: W Publishing, 2024), 138.

Session 6, Day 3

1. Lisa Whittle, *Put Your Warrior Boots On: Walking Jesus Strong, Once and for All* (Eugene, OR: Harvest House, 2017), 160.

Session 6, Day 5

1. Whittle, *I Want God*, 154.

Also available from Bible Teacher and best-selling author

Lisa Whittle

Every day we're bombarded with messages about our bodies: Fix this, change that. But what if we stopped seeing our bodies as projects to perfect, and instead understood and embraced them as God's incredible design? In Body and Soul, Lisa Whittle helps you discover how your body reflects the image of God and how your whole self– heart, mind, and body– matters deeply to Him.

LEARN MORE ABOUT LISA'S BOOKS AND BIBLE STUDIES:
WWW.LISAWHITTLE.COM